Essential Histories

The Peloponnesian War
431–404 BC

Essential Histories

The Peloponnesian War
431–404 BC

Philip de Souza

First published in Great Britain in 2002 by Osprey Publishing,
Elms Court, Chapel Way, Botley, Oxford OX2 9LP, UK.
Email: info@ospreypublishing.com

ISBN 1 84176 357 8

Editor: Rebecca Cullen
Design: Ken Vail Graphic Design, Cambridge, UK
Cartography by The Map Studio
Index by Bob Munro
Picture research by Image Select International
Origination by Grasmere Digital Imaging, Leeds, UK
Printed and bound in China by L. Rex Printing Company Ltd.

02 03 04 05 06   10 9 8 7 6 5 4 3 2 1

For a complete list of titles available from Osprey Publishing
please contact:

Osprey Direct UK, PO Box 140,
Wellingborough, Northants, NN8 2FA, UK.
Email: info@ospreydirect.co.uk

Osprey Direct USA, c/o MBI Publishing,
PO Box 1, 729 Prospect Ave,
Osceola, WI 54020, USA.
Email: info@ospreydirectusa.com

www.ospreypublishing.com

Dedication
For Debra

Author's Preface

This book was written under exceptionally difficult
circumstances. I am enormously grateful to Rebecca Cullen for
her understanding and patience. I am once more indebted to my
wife Debra for her love and support.

Contents

Introduction

This book gives a concise account of one of the key periods of Classical Greek history. The Peloponnesian War, which lasted from 431 to 404 BC, was a conflict between the Greek city-states of Athens and Sparta. It was a confrontation between the leading land power of the time, Sparta, and the leading sea power, Athens. In a wider sense it was also a clash between a cautious, traditional oligarchy and an ambitious, innovative democracy. It is called the Peloponnesian War because Sparta was the head of an alliance of Greek states from the Peloponnese, the southernmost peninsula of mainland Greece. The stories of the Peloponnesian War feature some of the great personalities of the Classical World, including the revered Athenian statesman Perikles, the bold and resourceful Spartans Brasidas and Gylippos, the flamboyant Athenian general Alkibiades and the Spartan leader Lysandros, who eventually achieved the decisive naval victory that the Spartans needed to win the war.

The enduring fame of the Peloponnesian War is due in no small way to its principal historian, Thucydides, an Athenian citizen who took part in some of the early stages of the war as a naval commander. He was exiled from Athens in 424 and he decided to write a detailed account of the war because, in his view, it was such an important war that it was more worthy of a written history than any previous conflict. He carefully gathered as much information as possible, from eye-witnesses and documents, so that he could offer as accurate and well considered an analysis of events as possible. He was aware that this sort of history might not appeal to those who preferred a more romanticised and sensational account of the past, but he observed in his introduction: 'This is a possession for all time, rather than a prize piece that is read and then forgotten.'

Thucydides' work is incomplete, tailing off literally in mid sentence, just as he is explaining what happened after an Athenian naval victory in 411. It is likely that he had either died, or at least stopped working on it by 396 because he does not seem to know about an eruption of Mount Etna on Sicily that occurred in this year. We do not know whether he simply had not written any of the remaining books which would have covered the period 410 to 404 (there were probably to be two more), or whether he had drafts or notes but no final versions.

Another Athenian historian, Xenophon, continued the story of the war from a point just a few months after the latest events recorded by Thucydides. This could imply that Xenophon had a version of Thucydides' work which was slightly longer than the one which now survives, for it seems clear that he intended his to be a continuation of Thucydides', although he is less detailed and analytical than Thucydides. Xenophon called his work the *Hellenika*, meaning an account of the doings of the Hellenes, which was the Greeks' name for themselves. We can supplement these two main accounts from the works of many later classical writers, who provide biographical and historical details not mentioned by Thucydides or Xenophon, along with a small number of original documents from the time of the war, mostly decrees of the Athenians inscribed on stone.

Thucydides was the first writer who, in explaining the origins of a war, made a clear distinction between the immediate, publicly proclaimed reasons for the conflict and the longer-term, underlying causes of tension between the two sides. This explanatory scheme is still regularly employed by modern historians when they seek to account for the outbreak of more recent wars. It is a testament to the fascination of Thucydides' subject and the quality of his work that, even in the twenty-first century, students of history, politics and warfare in universities and military academies across the world regularly study the events of the Peloponnesian War for the lessons it can teach them about politics, diplomacy, strategy, tactics and the writing of history.

This helmet was worn by a Greek heavy infantry soldier, or hoplite in the sixth century. By the start of the fifth century the city-states of Classical Greece had already fought many small scale wars, mostly as the result of border disputes with their neighbours. The Peloponnesian War was on a much grander scale than anything the Greeks had previously seen. (Ancient Art and Architecture)

Chronology

[AUTHOR'S NOTE ON DATES: All dates are BC. The official Athenian year, which was used by Thucydides and Xenophon as their main dating device, began and ended in midsummer. As a result some of the dates in this book are given in the form 416/15, which indicates the Athenian year that began in the summer of 416 and ended in the summer of 415]

The rise of Athens

The origins of the Peloponnesian War lie in the rise to power of its two protagonists, the city states of Athens and Sparta and their political estrangement during the middle part of the fifth century BC. Athens and Sparta had been the two leading states in the alliance of Greek city-states formed to combat the Persian king's invasion in 480. Both could claim to have been instrumental in saving the Greeks from conquest by the Persians, since the Athenians had taken the leading role in the naval victory over the Persians at Salamis in 480, but the following year the Spartans led the Greek army that defeated King Xerxes' land forces and ended the threat of Persian conquest.

After the Persians had been driven out of mainland Greece the alliance began to break up. The Spartan regent Pausanias led a victorious expedition to liberate Greek cities in the Eastern Aegean from the Persians, but he behaved with great arrogance and his treatment of the Eastern Greeks angered many of them. The Spartans recalled Pausanias and withdrew from the war against the Persians, leaving the alliance bereft of leadership. The Athenians were invited by several of the leading Greek states, particularly the cities and islands of Ionia, to lead them in a continuation of the war against the Persians. In 477 they created a new alliance to ravage the territory of the Persian king in compensation for the subjugation of the Ionians and the invasion of Greece. Each of the allies agreed to contribute men, ships or money to a common pool of resources which was administered and commanded by the Athenians. This alliance is called the Delian League by modern historians because its official treasury was established at the sanctuary of Apollo on the tiny island of Delos, in the centre of the Cyclades.

This painted water jug was produced in Athens after the Peloponnesian War. It shows a Greek hoplite (heavy infantryman) and an archer fighting a cavalryman who is dressed as a Persian. The hoplite carries a large, round shield on his left arm and uses a spear of between eight and 10 feet in length. Aside from his essential helmet he wears no other armour. (Ancient Art and Architecture)

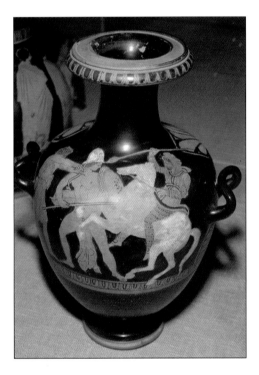

The Spartans already had their own alliance known as the Peloponnesian League. It was made up mainly of the small city-states in the Peloponnese, but some larger ones, such as Corinth, belonged, as did most of the cities of Boiotia, the region to the north of Athens. They had far greater autonomy than the members of the Delian League and they could vote on equal terms with the Spartans in the League conferences. It was essentially a defensive alliance that was only activated when there was a clear threat to the security of one or more of its members.

A bronze statue of Athena, patron goddess of the Athenians c. 450. The statue shows Athena wearing a hoplite's helmet. Her right arm originally held a spear and on her left can be seen the remnant of a strap for a large, round hoplite shield. The base bears an inscription saying, 'Melisso dedicated this as a tithe to Athena.' (Ancient Art and Architecture)

The Athenian Empire

The Delian League successfully waged war against the Persians, culminating in a magnificent victory under the command of the Athenian general Kimon at the Eurymedon river in 466. A Persian fleet of 200 ships was destroyed and with it the main threat to the security of the Greeks in the Aegean. In 459 the Delian League sent 200 ships to the Nile Delta to assist in an Egyptian revolt against the Persians, but four years later this revolt was crushed and the whole League force was lost. Kimon had been exiled in 461 but he returned in 451 to lead further campaigns, including an invasion of the Persian held island of Cyprus, where he died in 449. Later that year the Athenians negotiated a formal peace treaty with Persia, known as the Peace of Kallias.

The Delian League had proven a remarkably successful alliance in terms of its victories over the Persians and the security and prosperity it earned for its members, but what had started out as a League of Greek states under Athenian leadership gradually took on the character of an Athenian Empire. As early as 470 the Aegean island state of Naxos tried to opt out of its obligations, but was forced back into line. Its contribution to the League was changed from a certain number of ships for each campaign to a fixed annual 'tribute' of money, a process that was applied to more and more states. In 465 the island of Thasos tried to revolt; its citizens endured a two-year siege but eventually capitulated. They were reduced to tribute status and made to pay an indemnity, collected by the Athenians. In 454 the League's treasury was transferred to Athens. This move has made it possible for historians to study the finances of the League in some detail, because the Athenians gave one sixtieth of the annual tribute to their patron goddess Athena each year, recording the payments on stone slabs. Many of these so-called 'tribute lists' have survived and they show both the widening extent and the increasing wealth of the Athenian Empire. Allied revolts were put down with considerable ferocity and in some cases the Athenians appropriated land from the recalcitrant allies and established colonies of Athenian citizens there, to act in part as garrisons.

Inscribed records of decisions of the Athenian Assembly routinely refer to the allies as 'the cities which the Athenians rule'. Athens dominated the economic life of her subject allies, particularly their maritime trade. Some of the profits of the Empire were spent on the Athenian navy, on pay for Athenian citizens who carried out public offices and, it was rumoured among the other Greeks, the magnificent public buildings which adorned the city of Athens from the 440s onwards.

The 'First' Peloponnesian War

The major turning point in relations between the Athenians and the Spartans came in 462 BC. Two years earlier an earthquake had devastated Sparta, killing thousands. It sparked off a major revolt among the Helots of Lakonia and Messenia, who were servile populations under direct Spartan rule. Some of the Messenians successfully resisted Spartan attempts to bring them to heel and established themselves on Mount Ithome in Messenia. In 462, in response to a Spartan appeal to all her allies for help, Kimon persuaded the Athenians that he should lead a small army to assist them. Kimon and his force had not been in Messenia for very long when they, alone of all the allies whom the Spartans had invited to help them, were dismissed. The reason for this seems to have been a growing sympathy for the Messenians' cause among the Athenians.

Kimon was exiled on his return by the Athenians, who felt humiliated and insulted by the Spartans' actions. From 460 to 446 there was constant political tension between the two sides, with both Athens and Sparta forming alliances with each other's enemies. In some cases the tension resulted in a series of military conflicts which exacerbated the rivalry. These conflicts are sometimes called the First Peloponnesian War, although to some extent they lack the continuity and coherence which is characteristic of a single war.

In the fifth century BC, the Greeks felt that going to war in order to resolve a dispute or assert a claim to something was a right and proper thing to do. This certainly did not mean that they always resorted to violence in order to settle arguments, but the attempt to decide matters by armed force was accepted as a normal way of behaving for communities and states. If a state was felt to deserve punishment, it was not unusual for the inhabitants to be sold into slavery; in extreme cases the men might all be executed. Given the small size of most individual states, it was natural that treaties for mutual defence against third parties were regularly made, with each side promising to come to the aid of the other in the event of an attack. A common formula for such alliances was that both parties agreed to have the same friends and enemies.

One of the first things the Athenians did to vent their anger against the Spartans, therefore, was to make an alliance in 460 with Argos, Sparta's most powerful neighbour in the Peloponnese and her long-standing enemy. They also took advantage of a border dispute between their western neighbour, Megara, and her neighbour Corinth to detach Megara from the Peloponnesian League. To make Megara more secure from attack the Athenians built fortifications which linked the port of Nisaia to the city of Megara proper. The Athenians were acting out of self-interest in strengthening Megara. A Peloponnesian attack on their own territory would probably have to come through the Megarians' territory, known as the Megarid; an Athenian garrison was established in Megara. In 459 the Athenians began building their own fortifications, known as the Long Walls, to link the city of Athens to its main port at Peiraieus.

Another Athenian alliance, with the Thessalians, improved both their military and strategic position. The extensive open plains of Thessaly were ideal country for breeding and training horses, so the Thessalians were among the best cavalrymen in the Greek world, whereas mountainous Attika did not suit the breeding of horses and produced few cavalrymen. The Thessalians were also the northern neighbours of the Boiotians, whose southern borders with the Athenians were the subject of several disputes. In Thessaly and Megara the Athenians saw opportunities to weaken the Spartans by putting pressure on their allies.

In 457 the first major clash between the two sides occurred. The Peloponnesians bypassed Megara by taking their army by sea across the Gulf of Corinth. They encountered an Athenian army at Tanagra in Boiotia. The ranks of the Athenians were swelled to over 14,000 men by their allies, including 1,000 Argives, a large contingent from the Ionian states of the Delian League and a force of Thessalian cavalry. The Spartans and their allies numbered less than 12,000, but after two days of heavy fighting, during which the Thessalians changed sides, the Spartans won a prestigious victory. Once they had returned to the Peloponnese, however, the Athenians defeated the Boiotians in a separate battle at nearby Oinophyta, gaining control over much of central Greece as a result.

In 456 the Athenian general Tolmides took a force of 50 ships and, stopping at Gytheion on the coast of Lakonia, burnt the Spartan's dockyard facilities. The Athenians also ravaged some of the surrounding

territory, then headed north into the Corinthian Gulf, capturing the Corinthian-held city of Chalkis on the northern shore of the narrow entrance to the Gulf. This expedition demonstrated the strategic advantage of Athens' massive fleet. A more significant outcome, however, was the capture of the small city of Naupaktos, also on the northern shore of the Gulf of Corinth. Here the Athenians established a large group of Messenians who had been allowed to leave by the Spartans as the only way of ending the Messenian revolt. They were to play a major role in the future confrontations between Athens and Sparta. The Athenians made more sorties north to punish the Thessalians for their treachery at Tanagra and in 454 they sailed into the Corinthian Gulf once more to discourage naval activity by the Corinthians and harry their allies and friends in Western Greece. But the destruction of the Athenian expedition to Egypt, increasing difficulties in

This model shows an Athenian trireme at rest in one of the specially constructed ship-sheds around the Peiraieus. As well as the ships and their crews a Greek city needed to invest in substantial facilities in order to maintain an effective navy. For many of the cities in the Delian League the cost was too great, so they contributed money rather than ships to the League's war efforts. (J F Coates)

A sixth-century black-figure Athenian painted vase showing two warriors
fighting. Although Greek armies regularly consisted of several thousand
men, artists preferred to paint scenes of individual duels in the tradition of
the Greek heroes of the Homeric epic the *Iliad*. (Ashmolean Museum)

Scenes of parting like this one are quite common on Athenian painted pottery from the fifth century. Athens and her allies were at war with Persia or their fellow Greeks almost continually from the Persian invasion of 480 to the conclusion of the Thirty Years' peace in 446. (Ancient Art and Architecture)

controlling the Athenian Empire, and the reluctance of the Spartans to venture out of the Peloponnese reduced the belligerence of both sides. A five-year truce was agreed in 451, as well as a Thirty Years' Peace between Sparta and Argos.

In 446 the Boiotians began to agitate against Athenian domination and a punitive expedition led by Tolmides was defeated at Koroneia, with many Athenians taken captive. In order to secure their safe return Athens abandoned all of Boiotia except the southern city of Plataia. A federal political structure was created by the Boiotians, with their largest city, Thebes, taking a leading role. This move inspired the island of Euboia to revolt from Athens. While the Athenians were trying to suppress the Euboians, the Megarians, encouraged by Corinth and Sikyon, also revolted, killing their Athenian garrisons, and the young Spartan king Pleistoanax led the army of the Peloponnesian League into the Megarid to consolidate the revolt of Megara. The Athenian general Perikles rushed his forces back from Euboia to confront Pleistoanax, who had reached Eleusis. The Spartan king withdrew without any attempt at battle, leaving Perikles free to return to Euboia and suppress the revolt. There were accusations that he had bribed the Spartan king and Pleistoanax's senior adviser, Kleandridas, was

This photograph shows an impression taken from one of the huge stones on which the Athenians recorded the dedication of $1/60$ of their annual tribute to the goddess Athena. By studying the details of these 'tribute lists' historians have discovered how some of the cities that revolted from the Delian League were punished through loss of territory and the imposition of colonies of Athenian settlers, which resulted in their payments being reduced. (Archive of Squeezes, Oxford)

Athens and Peiraeus during the war

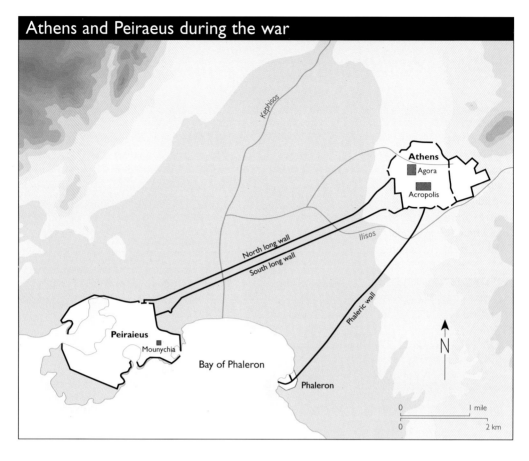

condemned to death for treason and forced into exile to avoid execution. He eventually settled in Thurii, an Athenian colony in Southern Italy, where he became a leading military commander and was influential in bringing the city into an alliance with the Peloponnesians in 435. Pleistoanax himself was tried and acquitted, but he nevertheless went into exile as well.

In 446 the Athenians agreed a peace treaty with the Spartans, to last for 30 years. Its terms were that each side should retain its territory and alliances. Athens gave up any claim over Boiotia and agreed to stop trying to expand her empire at the expense of the Peloponnesian states, but she kept control of Naupaktos. An important clause in the treaty provided for independent arbitration of any disputes that might arise over the observance of its terms. The mutual dislike and

suspicion which had caused the 'First' Peloponnesian War was not dispelled by the Thirty Years' Peace, however, and both sides continued to look for ways to disadvantage each other. When the island of Samos in the Eastern Aegean revolted against Athens with Persian help in 441, the Spartans tried to take advantage of this and go to war with Athens, but at a meeting in 440 they could not persuade a majority of members of Peloponnesian League to vote with them. Nevertheless there was a growing sense among the Greeks that a decisive confrontation between Athens and Sparta was looming. In the historian Thucydides' view, although there were several short-term justifications for the main Peloponnesian War, it was 'the increasing magnitude of Athenian power and the fear this caused to the Spartans that forced them into war.'

Athens and Sparta

In the fifth century BC Greece was divided into hundreds of independent city-states; the Greek word for this type of state was *polis* (plural *poleis*). The size of these states varied considerably, but most comprised an urban centre, where much of the population lived, and where the principal public buildings were located, plus a surrounding rural territory. Although there were many differences in the ways that each state was organised and governed, broadly speaking they came in two types: either a democracy, where decision making was in the hands of the majority of the citizens, or an oligarchy, in which effective control of decision making was limited to a minority of the citizens.

Greece in the Peloponnesian War 431–404

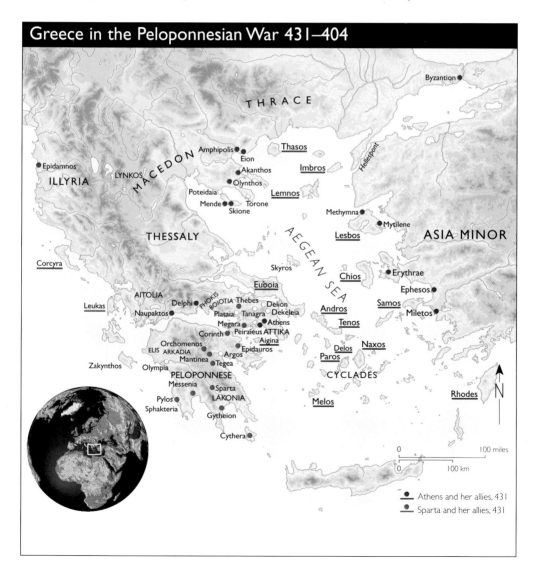

Byzantion

THRACE

Epidamnos

ILLYRIA

LYNKOS

MACEDON

Amphipolis
Eion
Akanthos
Olynthos
Poteidaia
Mende Torone
Skione

Thasos

Imbros

Hellespont

Lemnos

Methymna
Mytilene

THESSALY

Lesbos

ASIA MINOR

Corcyra

AEGEAN SEA

Skyros

Chios
Erythrae
Ephesos

Euboia

AITOLIA

Leukas
Naupaktos

Delphi
PHOKIS
BOIOTIA Thebes
Plataia Tanagra Delion
Megara Dekeleia
Corinth Peiraieus ATTIKA
Athens
Aigina

Andros
Samos
Miletos

Tenos

Orchomenos
ELIS ARKADIA
Mantinea
Zakynthos Olympia
Argos
Tegea
Epidauros

Delos
Paros
Naxos

PELOPONNESE
Messenia Sparta
Pylos LAKONIA
Sphakteria
Gytheion

CYCLADES

Melos

Rhodes

N

Cythera

0   100 miles
0   100 km

●— Athens and her allies, 431
○— Sparta and her allies, 431

Athens

Athens was a relatively large state comprising the peninsula of Attika, with the city of Athens as its political and religious centre. The Athenians had a very broadly based, democratic constitution. The major decisions were taken by the Assembly, attendance at which was open to all adult male citizens. The Assembly met regularly to debate proposals on important issues put before it by a committee, but anyone who wanted to could speak out in a debate, or make their own proposal, as long as it was not contrary to one that had already been voted into law. The Assembly could not meet every day, so mundane financial and administrative matters and the day-to-day running of the state's affairs were in the hands of several smaller committees. The most important of these was the Council, consisting of 500 men who were selected by lot from citizens over the age of 30. It was the Council that prepared the agenda for meetings of the Assembly. A sub-committee of 50 members of the Council was permanently on duty each month, living in a special building next to the Council chamber. Membership of the Council and the other committees changed every year, which meant that there were plenty of opportunities for ordinary citizens to participate in government.

Although in theory any Athenian citizen was entitled to speak out in the Assembly, in practice meetings tended to be dominated by a handful of individuals. These politicians were often men of aristocratic birth, whose wealth, education, family connections and military experience commanded respect among the ordinary citizens. Kimon, the leader of several successful Delian League expeditions against the Persian Empire was one such figure, but the most influential politician in the mid-fifth century was Perikles, the son of Xanthippos. As well as being rich, well bred and a good military commander, Perikles was an excellent orator. He was able to persuade the citizens in the Assembly to elect him as a general year after year and to vote in favour of his proposals for using the political power and financial resources of the Athenian Empire for the benefit of the poorer citizens. After Perikles' death in 429 many other politicians competed for popularity and influence over the Athenians, but none ever managed to attain such a dominant position again.

A photograph of the remains of the Athenian Acropolis. The rocky outcrop in the middle of Athens had been a citadel and a sanctuary for many centuries and had several temples. Around 447 Pericles persuaded the Athenians to transform it by building a monumental set of marble buildings which were to be the most magnificent in the Greek world. They served as potent symbols of the wealth, power and pride of the Athenians. (Ancient Art and Architecture)

Sparta

Sparta was the name of the city in the centre of the fertile territory of Lakonia (also called Lakedaimon). Unlike Athens Sparta had few monumental buildings and it was essentially a loose amalgamation of five villages. The Spartans had gradually evolved a system that combined monarchical and democratic elements within an oligarchy. Over the preceding centuries most of the Greek states had expelled their kings, or reduced them to purely ceremonial functions, but the Spartans retained two kings who acted as leaders in warfare and religious matters. In most respects, however, Sparta was a typical oligarchy, with its public business in the hands of a few men. Major decisions were referred to an assembly of adult male citizens, but there was little or no chance for the ordinary citizens to discuss or debate them. They were simply expected to indicate their agreement or disagreement with what their leaders suggested. Debates on important issues were restricted to smaller groups of elected officials. Every year the Spartans elected a board of five overseers or *ephors*, who had wide ranging executive, disciplinary and judicial powers over all the people of Lakonia, including the two kings. Although they were not subject to any written laws and they had the authority to prosecute any Spartan citizen, regardless of their official status, the ephors were only in power for a year and they could not be re-elected at any time.

The Spartans did not have a deliberative council that routinely discussed all public business, as the Athenian Council of 500 did. Instead they had a council of senior citizens, called the *gerousia*, whose 28 members were elected by their fellow citizens for life, but they normally did not achieve this status until they were over 60 years of age. This high age limit is not particularly surprising given the ancient Greeks' traditional respect for age and experience. Men who had reached 60 were considered to be in physical decline, and so no longer suited for the rigours of warfare, but still in full possession of their mental faculties. The main function of the members of the *gerousia* was to oversee observance of Sparta's laws and customs, particularly in relation to the upbringing and discipline of citizens. They could act as a consultative body for the kings and the ephors on major public decisions, although there is no clear evidence as to their role in determining foreign policy. They discussed and prepared proposals which were put before the assembly of Spartan citizens, and they acted as a court for political trials, or inquests into the conduct of kings and other leading Spartans. The two kings were also members of the *gerousia*. They could exercise a leading role in its deliberations through informal ties of patronage and friendship with its members.

An interesting difference in the way the citizen assemblies of Athens and Sparta operated was that, whereas the Athenians assessed the size of a majority by counting raised hands, the Spartans judged decisions on the basis of how loudly the assembled citizens shouted in favour of a proposal, or a candidate for election. Such a method was less precise and the outcome could be more easily manipulated by the presiding magistrates. It is indicative of a strong reluctance among the members of the ruling oligarchy to allow the citizen body to have true sovereignty over public affairs. This antipathy towards full democracy, as practised by the Athenians and many of their allies, was one of the fundamental causes of tension between the two sides.

Military hierarchies

The command structures of the two sides also reveal a lot about their different political and social systems. Athenian armies were usually commanded by one or more members of a board of 10 generals, who were elected annually by the citizens. Successful generals, like Kimon or Perikles, were often re-elected and they exploited their popularity and prestige to play a leading role in Athenian politics, whereas unsuccessful, or unpopular generals would not be re-elected. The generals could be held to account for their actions by the Assembly, which sometimes acted as a court sitting in judgment over

The two men on this Spartan relief are probably citizens. The Spartans prided themselves on their constant readiness to fight for their city. They were expected to value their city and their comrades above themselves and their families. Until the age of 30 they did not even live in their own homes, but stayed in their mess halls and visited their wives occasionally. (Ancient Art and Architecture)

them. Even the great Perikles suffered the humiliation of being deposed and fined early on in the war because the Athenians did not regard his strategy as being successful. The ultimate sovereignty of the Athenian citizens over their generals tended to have an inhibiting effect on their actions.

The full Spartan army could only be commanded by one of the kings, or a regent if the kings were unable to take command in person. The kings were accompanied on campaign by two ephors,

A Roman bust of Perikles based on an Athenian original. Perikles was so good at persuading the Athenians to vote for his proposals that the historian Thucydides felt that although the Athens of his time was called a democracy, in fact it was ruled by its leading citizen. (Ancient Art and Architecture)

but the kings seem to have exercised complete authority while the army was on active service. The ephors could, however, prosecute the kings before a court consisting of themselves and the *gerousia*, if they considered that they had acted inappropriately while in command of the army. During the Peloponnesian War the full Spartan army rarely took the field. Instead one of the kings led armies consisting of a small proportion of Spartan

This Athenian vase depicts a soldier taking leave of his family as he goes off to war. It was part of the public duty of an Athenian citizen to fight when called upon. Normally it was only the fairly prosperous citizens who could afford the equipment of a hoplite. The poorer citizens were more likely to serve as oarsmen or sailors in the fleet. (Ancient Art and Architecture)

citizens, along with the combined forces of their Peloponnesian League allies on campaigns in Southern and Central Greece. For expeditions further afield they sent much smaller Spartan detachments, led by specially appointed Spartan officers. These men were allowed a great deal of latitude in deciding how to conduct their operations, but internal rivalries and jealousies were commonplace among the Spartans. At several points during the war successful commanders were refused reinforcements or prevented from carrying on their achievements because other Spartans did not want them to gain too much prestige.

Athenian manpower

It has been estimated that the total number of adult male Athenian citizens in 431 was around 40,000. Of these about 1,000 were wealthy enough to serve as cavalrymen, which involved maintaining their own horses. Of the rest as many as 20,000 may have been eligible to serve as hoplites, the heavily armed infantrymen who usually formed the core of a Greek citizen army, but less than half of them would be called upon to fight at any one time. In practice the forces that Athens mobilised during the war were composed of her own citizens and those of her allies, supplemented by mercenaries. Athens commanded fleets and armies drawn from her Delian League allies many times during the fifth century but only on a few occasions are we able to get a clear idea of the proportions of Athenian to allied forces involved in the campaigns of the Peloponnesian War. The most detailed breakdown is provided by Thucydides when he describes the forces sent on an expedition to Sicily in 415. There were 5,100 hoplites, or heavy infantrymen, of whom 2,200 were Athenian citizens, 750 were mercenaries from the Peloponnese, and the remaining 2,150 were supplied by Athens' subject allies of the Delian League. The fleet of 134 trireme warships was made up of 100 Athenian vessels and 34 from the

allies, principally the large and populous island of Chios. It is unlikely that the allies regularly contributed as many as half of the soldiers involved in all the military undertakings of the Peloponnesian War. Athens despatched troops to many parts of the Greek world during the war and often there will have been only a few allied soldiers involved, mostly serving as mercenaries.

Naval manpower requirements were on a far larger scale. Few cities, even one a populous as Athens, had the necessary resources to man a large fleet, since a trireme normally required 150-170 oarsmen, plus skilled sailors and steersmen, who were especially hard to find. In 433, for example, when the Corinthians were preparing a major expedition against Corcyra, they offered very generous rates of pay to potential rowers from all over the Greek world in a desperate attempt to recruit enough oarsmen to man their ships. Similarly, it was vital for the Athenians to be able to recruit from as wide a pool of naval manpower as possible and they had to pay recruits well enough to prevent them from deserting to the other side, or returning home.

Spartan manpower

Male Spartan citizens (*Spartiates* in Greek) were almost constantly in training as hoplites. They did not have any other occupation and their farmland was worked for them by slaves. Their training began at a very early age, usually five or six years and continued through various stages until, at 18 years' old, they were allowed to attend meetings of the citizen assembly and go abroad on military expeditions. At this age they were admitted to a mess group (the Greek word for which is *syssition*). Each mess group was made up of about 15 Spartans who trained, exercised, dined and fought together. In theory they were all of equal status and contributed food and other resources to a common stock of supplies. If they could not afford to make their regular contributions they could be deprived of their full citizen status.

The total number of full Spartan citizens was never very large. Even when it was at its greatest extent, towards the end of the sixth century BC, it was probably less than 10,000, and by the start of the Peloponnesian War there may have been only half that number of adult male citizens available for military service. So from where did the Spartans obtain the manpower for their armies? To some extent they relied upon the non-Spartan population of Lakonia, especially those men who lived in the towns and villages around Sparta and were called the *Perioikoi*, which means 'dwellers around'. The Perioikoi lived in autonomous communities, some of which were large towns or even small cities. Unlike the Spartans they worked for a living, as farmers, traders and craftsmen. It was the Perioikoi who made the armour and weapons used by Spartans as well as day-to-day items like pottery, furniture and cloth. Usually they fought as hoplites alongside the Spartans themselves.

When they needed to assemble a large army to take on another Greek state, like Athens or Argos, the Spartans called upon the allied states of the Peloponnesian League. The nearest of these were the cities of Arkadia, the mountainous region to the north and west of Lakonia. The main Arkadian cities of Orchomenos, Tegea and Mantinea were not very large, but each of them could easily muster several hundred soldiers. Larger contingents were contributed by more distant states like Corinth and Thebes. These allies probably provided the majority of hoplites in any Spartan army, especially when serving outside of the Peloponnese.

The Helot curse

The Spartans also made considerable use of the large, publicly owned, slave population of Lakonia and its neighbouring region,

Messenia. These slaves were called *Helots* and they were the descendants of people who were conquered and enslaved by the Spartans in a series of wars from about 950 to 700 BC. The Messenians proved very difficult to control and organised major revolts against the Spartans on several occasions. The Helots of Lakonia were less rebellious and substantial numbers of them normally accompanied the Spartans to war, acting as baggage carriers and fighting as light armed soldiers. During the Peloponnesian War they were used as oarsmen and sailors on Spartan naval vessels. In exceptional circumstances Helots were equipped and trained to fight as hoplites, on the understanding that they would be given their freedom at the end of the campaign for which they were recruited.

An important feature of the Spartan system for maintaining discipline and obedience was the regular use of physical violence. From the start of their boyhood training Spartans were beaten by their elders and superiors. Spartan citizens were especially encouraged to use violence against the Helots. Each year the Spartan ephors declared a ritual war on the Helots, thus justifying the killing of any troublesome Helots and keeping the rest in a constant state of fear. Yet for all their heavy-handed domination and control of the Helots, the Spartans could not do without them. It was the labour of the Helots that furnished the individual Spartan citizens with natural products for their contributions to the communal messes.

Throughout the Classical period the Spartans' main priority was always to keep their dominant position over the Helots, who were so essential to their own way of life. But this was no easy task, even for men who were constantly prepared for war. The Messenian revolt of 462–456 showed how fragile the Spartans' control was, and the abrupt dismissal of Kimon and his Athenian contingent indicates how sensitive Spartans were to any interference in their relationship with the Messenians. The

This bronze statuette of a hoplite was probably made in Lakonia and dedicated by a Spartan citizen at the sanctuary of Zeus in Olympia. The Spartans were famous for their zealous observance of religious rituals. Many similar offerings have been found in sanctuaries around the Peloponnese and elsewhere in Greece. (Ancient Art and Architecture)

continual need to subjugate this conquered population was the main reason why the Spartans were reluctant to commit large numbers of citizens to campaigns outside the Peloponnese. In the words of the modern scholar Geoffrey de Sainte Croix, who studied the history of the Peloponnesian War in great detail: 'The Helot danger was the curse Sparta had brought upon herself, an admirable illustration of the maxim that a people which oppresses another cannot itself be free.'

Fear and suspicion lead to war

The most immediate, short-term cause of the Peloponnesian War, according to Thucydides, was the judgment of the Spartans, endorsed by their allies, that the Athenians had broken the terms of the Thirty Years' Peace. A key clause was a guarantee that no state would be deprived of its autonomy. This did not mean that the Athenians could not demand tribute from their subject allies, nor that the Spartans had to relinquish control over the Peloponnesian League. Rather it meant that no state should be deprived of the freedom to run its own affairs, insofar as it had done before the peace treaty was agreed. The Athenians were accused of failing to respect this clause by several of the Greek states.

The case against Athens

The Spartans were under considerable pressure from their allies in the Peloponnesian League to restrain the Athenians. In 432 they invited all interested parties to put their case before a meeting of the Spartan Assembly. Prominent among the states arguing for war was Corinth. There were two main Corinthian complaints. One was the action of Athens on behalf of Corcyra (modern Corfu) against the Corinthians. In 435 the Corinthian colony of Corcyra was involved in a dispute with her colony at Epidamnos, in modern Albania. This dispute escalated to involve the Corinthians, on the side of Epidamnos, in a naval battle in 432 with the Athenians, who had made a defensive alliance with Corcyra in 433. Corcyra had a large navy of her own and the Corinthians and other Peloponnesians feared that their alliance might make the Athenians invincible at sea. They also saw the Athenians' involvement as unjustifiable interference in their affairs, contrary to the terms of the Thirty Years' Peace.

The other Corinthian complaint was over Athens' treatment of the city of Poteidaia. This city, located on the westernmost spur of the Chalkidike peninsula, had originally been founded by Corinthians and still received its annual magistrates from Corinth. It was a tribute-paying member of the Delian League and of great strategic importance because of its proximity to the territory of the Macedonian king, Perdikkas, who was a former ally of Athens. Perdikkas was now encouraging the cities of Chalkidike to revolt from Athens. They had formed a league with its political and economic centre at Olynthos. The Poteidaians had been ordered by Athens to send their Corinthian magistrates back home and dismantle their fortifications. While they negotiated with the Athenians they sent an embassy to the Peloponnese and obtained an assurance from Sparta that if the Athenians attacked Poteidaia, Sparta would invade Attika. The Athenians were fearful that they might lose control of this prosperous area, which provided some seven per cent of their tribute revenue, so they sent forces to lay siege to the city, which had been reinforced by troops from Corinth and mercenaries from the Peloponnese. The Corinthians complained that Athens was breaking the terms of the Peace and demanded that the Spartans invade Attika.

A further complaint against Athens was made by the people of Megara, who complained that they had been excluded from access to the harbours and market-place of Athens by a decree of the Athenian Assembly. The purpose of what is known as the Megarian decree seems to have been to put pressure on the Megarians to abandon their alliance with Sparta and the Peloponnesians and resume their alliance with Athens, which they had abandoned in 446. The Megarians' territory

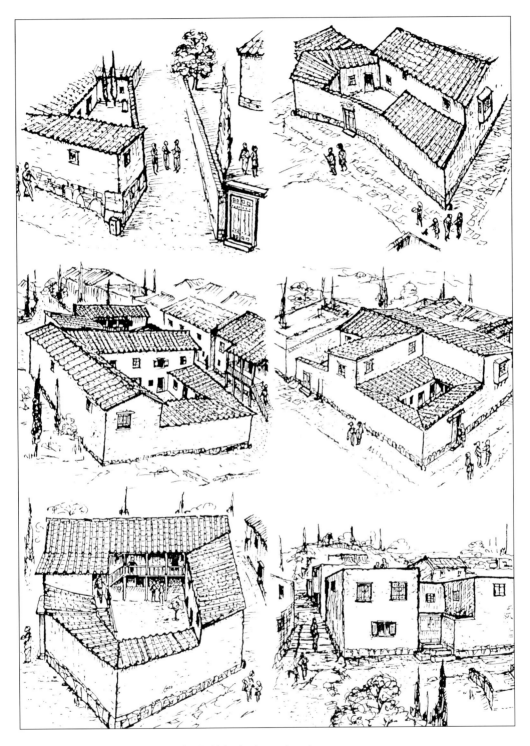

These sketches show reconstructions of typical Athenian houses based on
archeological remains. The walls were built of sun-dried clay bricks and the
roofs were covered with large pottery tiles. The windows had no glass, only
wooden shutters. Most houses were built around a small courtyard and those
of wealthier families would usually have an upper storey. (John Ellis Jones)

bordered on Attika in the east and provided potential access for a Peloponnesian army to attack Athens. The exclusions from Athenian harbours and markets seem to have had a very severe effect on Megarian trade. This is not surprising as Athens was the largest city in Greece and her commercial harbour at Peiraieus was a major centre of maritime trade.

Representatives from the island state of Aigina also complained that their autonomy was being infringed by Athens. Aigina had been part of the Athenian Empire since 458, but is not unlikely that the Athenians had recently begun to behave more aggressively towards Aiginetans for similar reasons to those which were causing them to put pressure on Megara. The Athenians must have been conscious of the fact that Aigina provided a potential base for naval attacks on Athens and her maritime trade. Autonomy was fine for some of the more distant islands or cities in the Aegean, but for places on their doorstep the Athenians preferred the same kind of close control as the Spartans exercised over their Messenian neighbours. An Athenian garrison was installed on the island by 432 and, although the Aiginetan tribute payments were reduced by over half, this meant an effective end to the Aiginetans' right to govern themselves freely, again contrary to the key clause of the Thirty Years' Peace.

The Athenians claimed that they had the right to do as they pleased regarding their empire, which they had won for themselves at considerable cost. They probably had not expected their treatment of Aigina to become an issue, given the fact that in the case of Samos in 440 the Corinthians themselves had upheld the right of Athens to police its own empire. In the case of Corcyra they felt that they were doing no more than responding to a defensive request from an ally, although it is unlikely that they entered into the alliance without some expectation of clashing with the Corinthians. They pointed out that Poteidaia was one of their tribute-paying allies and had been encouraged to revolt by the Corinthians, who were openly fighting against them on the side of the Poteidaians. The Megarian decree, they claimed, was

simply a set of religious sanctions imposed because the Megarians had cultivated some land which was supposed to be left untouched as it was sacred to the gods, as well as some disputed territory on the border between Attika and the Megarid. They also accused the Megarians of sheltering runaway Athenian slaves.

The Spartans and their allies vote for war

Having heard the complaints and the counter-arguments of the Athenians, the Spartans removed everyone except the full Spartan citizens from the assembly place so that they could discuss the matter among themselves. The vast majority of the Spartans were angered by what they had heard. Their allies had convinced them that the Athenians had broken the terms of the Thirty Years' Peace and were acting with unreasonable aggression. In consequence there was great enthusiasm for immediately declaring war on Athens. At this point one of the two kings, Archidamos, introduced a note of caution. He seems to have argued that it was premature of the Spartans to rush into war a with Athens, whose extensive empire provided her with the resources to fight a protracted war more easily than the Spartans. He pointed out that Athens' chief strength lay in her naval power, while Sparta was essentially a land power. He advised sending diplomatic missions to try to seek negotiated settlements of the various disputes, while at the same time recruiting new allies, accumulating resources and preparing for a war in which expensive naval campaigns would be necessary to obtain victory. He had to put his arguments carefully, in order to avoid offending the Spartans' sense of duty towards their allies and their great pride in their martial prowess, whilst at the same time pointing out to them the true size of the task that lay before them. Thucydides' version of a key part of his speech is as follows:

No-one can call us cowards if, in spite of our numbers, we seem in no hurry to attack a single city. Their allies are no less numerous than ours and theirs contribute money. And in war it is the expenditure which enables the weapons to bring results, especially in a conflict between a land power and a sea power. Let us gather our resources first and not get rushed into premature action by the words of our allies. We shall have to bear the brunt of it all, however things turn out. So let us consider the options in a calm fashion.

In response to Archidamos' sensible and cautious arguments the ephor Sthenelaidas appealed to the sense of outrage at the Athenians' high-handed behaviour and exhorted the Spartans to take decisive action against them. Thucydides' version of his speech dismisses Archidamos' concerns over resources and emphasises the need to respond decisively to the demands of Sparta's allies:

For while the other side may have plenty of money, ships and horses, we have good allies whom we cannot betray to the Athenians. Nor is this something to be decided by diplomacy and negotiations; it's not through words that our interests are being harmed. Our vengeance must be strong and swift ... So vote as befits you Spartans, for war! Do not allow the Athenians to become stronger and do not utterly betray your allies! With the gods beside us let us challenge the unrighteous!

In spite of the fervour of his rhetoric, when Sthenelaidas, as the ephor presiding over the Spartan assembly, put the matter to a vote, he claimed that he could not tell whether the shouts were louder for or against going to war. So he told the Spartans to separate into two groups and then it was clear that the majority favoured war. All that remained was for the Spartans to call a congress of the Peloponnesian League to get their allies' approval for a war against the Athenians. The vote was not unanimous, but the Corinthians persuaded a majority of the Peloponnesians to declare that Athens

had broken the terms of the Thirty Years' Peace.

Even now the Spartans were reluctant to act. They sent an embassy to Athens to try to negotiate a settlement. The autonomy of Poteidaia and Aigina was raised in these discussions, but the main sticking point seems to have been the Megarian decree, which the Athenians refused to rescind. Eventually a Spartan envoy delivered the message, 'We want peace and we want the Athenians to let their allies be free.' Perikles told the Athenian Assembly that the Spartans could not be trusted to stop at these demands, but would try to force them to give up more and more in the name of freedom for the Greeks. He encouraged the Athenians to tell the Spartan envoys that they too should stop interfering in the affairs of their own allies, and submit the problem of supposed infringements of the Thirty Years' Peace to arbitration. At this point the Spartans abandoned the negotiations. As Thucydides stressed, the underlying cause of the war was Athens' growing power and the fear that caused among the Spartans and their allies. No amount of diplomacy would change the reality of that power or the fear that it was generating.

The Thebans strike first

The Boiotians also had grievances against the Athenians going back nearly 30 years. Plataia was the only Boiotian city which had not joined the Boiotian League, in which the Thebans were the dominant force. It is not entirely surprising, therefore, that the opening encounter of the Peloponnesian War was not a Spartan led invasion of Attika, but a pre-emptive strike on Plataia by the Thebans, who were anxious to secure as much of their border with Attika as possible. They were acting in concert with a group of Plataians who were unhappy with their city's long-standing alliance with Athens and wanted to bring it over to the Spartan side in line with most of the rest of Boiotia.

The majority of the Plataians were unaware of this plot and they were taken completely by surprise. When an advance force of around 300 Theban hoplites entered the city and told the Plataians that they should join the League of Boiotian cities, they were initially cowed, but once they realised that the rest of the Theban army had been delayed by heavy rain their anti-Theban and pro-Athenian feelings reasserted themselves. After a vicious struggle at night, in the pouring rain, which involved not just the Plataian citizens but many of their women and slaves, 120 Thebans were dead and the rest surrendered. The main strength of the Thebans did not arrive until later the next morning and they withdrew after being promised that the prisoners would not be harmed. The Athenians were told about the attack and sent a herald to urge the Plataians not to act rashly. By the time this message arrived, however, the Plataians had gathered all their property into the city and executed their Theban prisoners. There was now no doubt that the Thirty Years' Peace was over and Plataia was reinforced by the Athenians, who evacuated the women, children and men who were too old to fight. The attack on Plataia provided an early indication of the level of bloodshed which was to become commonplace in the Greek world over the next three decades.

The first twenty years

The Archidamian War

The first 10 years of conflict between Athens and Sparta were considered by many of the Greeks to have constituted a separate war. At the start of the war the Peloponnesian strategy was to invade the territory of Attika by land, damaging crops and buildings and forcing the Athenians to come out of their city and settle the war in a decisive pitched battle. The Peloponnesians were confident that they would win such a battle. If no such confrontation was achieved, the Peloponnesians hoped that the Athenian citizens would soon grow weary of the attacks and look for a settlement on terms favourable to their opponents. For the first few years the Peloponnesian army was led by the only available Spartan king, Archidamos, whose name is given by modern historians to this part of the war.

The Athenians also doubted their ability to defeat Sparta and her allies in a major hoplite confrontation, so, at the urging of Perikles, they retreated behind their fortifications and waited for the Peloponnesians to give up and go home. They struck back by using their superior naval forces to attack the territory of

The young man featured on this Athenian wine jug of about 430 BC is equipped with the typical large round shield, long spear and short sword of the hoplite. He wears no body armour, only a heavy tunic and a headband to ease the fit of his bronze helmet. The lion device on his shield is a personal one. At the start of the Peloponnesian War most Greek cities did not have standardised symbols for their soldiers, which sometimes caused confusion in battle. (Boston Museum of Fine Arts)

Sparta and her allies, hoping to make them lose their enthusiasm for the conflict. This strategy could not win them the war, but it could prolong the stalemate and might discourage enough of the enemy to force them to make peace. The strategists on both sides probably thought that there would be only a few years of fighting before a settlement was reached.

In fact the annual invasions of the Archidamian War, of which there were five between 431 and 425, did not always last very long, nor, indeed, did they succeed in doing much damage. Athenian cavalry harried the light troops on the Peloponnesian side and even the longest invasion, lasting 40 days in 430, failed to cause much harm. Athens could import much of its food, particularly grain, via the shipping routes secured by Athens' maritime empire and powerful navy. In any case it proved difficult to assemble the Peloponnesian forces at the right time to strike against Attika's agricultural resources, in part probably because many of the soldiers wanted to be at home on their own farmland. In 429 the Peloponnesians were persuaded by the Thebans to make a determined attempt to overcome the resistance of Plataia. The Spartan king Archidamos, conscious of the historical significance of Plataia as the site of Sparta's great victory over the Persians in 479, tried to negotiate a surrender, but assurances from the Athenians that they would not abandon the Plataians convinced those still inside the city walls to hold out. The Spartans built a circuit of wooden siege fortifications to prevent any forces from getting in to relieve the 600 or so remaining people. A breakout was achieved during a winter storm by about 200 men, who climbed over the walls using ladders, but they could not persuade the Athenians to send a force to relieve the siege.

In the summer of 426 the new Spartan king, Agis, son of Archidamos, was leading another expedition of Peloponnesian forces into the Isthmus of Corinth on their way to Attika when there was an earthquake, which forced them to turn back before they had even reached Athenian territory. In the following year a similar expedition, also led by Agis,

arrived in Attika early in the summer, when the crops were still a long way from ripening and the weather was very stormy. This made it difficult for the Spartans to feed themselves while they were camped on Athenian territory and the troops began to complain. Then news arrived of a serious Athenian incursion at Pylos on the western coast of the Peloponnese and the whole army was withdrawn, having stayed in Attika for only 15 days.

A devastating plague struck Athens in 430, with further outbreaks in 429 and 426. The second year it killed Perikles himself, but even this misery did not convince the Athenians to seek peace. If anything it probably made them keener to cause harm to their enemies in return and the scale and range of naval counter-strikes was stepped up after Perikles' death. The Peloponnesians themselves made limited use of their naval forces, which were principally furnished by the Corinthians. A grandiose scheme was hatched to involve the Western Greeks of Sicily and Southern Italy in the war and create a huge fleet of 500 triremes, but this came to nothing and the Athenians took the initiative in the west by sending expeditions to Sicily. They went at the invitation of an old ally, the city of Leontini, which asked for their help against the larger city of Syracuse. Two small Athenian fleets were sent to Sicily in 427 and 425, partly with the aim of disrupting grain supplies from the island to the Peloponnese, but also with an eye towards adding as much of the island as they could to the Athenian Empire. In 424, however, the Sicilian cities came to an understanding among themselves and the Athenians returned home without anything to show for their efforts.

The revolt of Mytilene and the end of Plataia

The next major setback of the war for the Athenians was a revolt in 428 on the island of Lesbos, led by the largest city, Mytilene. The cities of Lesbos had been founders of the Delian League and their contributions to its resources were crucial to the Athenian war effort. With the exception of Methymna they had oligarchic governments and they decided that in her severely weakened state Athens would not be able to respond effectively to an attempt to break away from her control. The Athenians despatched a small army and a fleet to blockade Mytilene, which was dependent on reinforcements and food supplies from overseas. The Mytileneans asked Sparta and the Peloponnesian League for help and a relief force was slowly assembled under the command of the Spartan Alkidas. The Athenians moved faster, however, sending a second fleet of 100 ships early in 427, in spite of the losses caused by the plague. The oligarchic regime at Mytilene distributed weapons to the mass of the population to stiffen their defences, but this plan backfired and the newly empowered citizens demanded a general distribution of grain to feed the starving population. When this did not materialise they surrendered the city to the Athenian commander Paches, who sent the leaders of the revolt back to Athens.

A debate ensued in the Athenian Assembly about the appropriate punishment for the Mytilenean rebels. The politician Kleon persuaded the citizens that an example had to be made of the people of Mytilene in order to discourage further revolts. He proposed that all the adult male citizens should be executed and the women and children sold into slavery. The Assembly voted in favour of this and despatched a ship to tell Paches to carry out this brutal decree. The next day, however, many people realised the injustice of the decision. A second meeting of the Assembly was called and the citizens voted to rescind their decree and only to punish those who were guilty of leading the revolt. A second trireme was sent out with the revised orders. Its crew rowed in shifts, not putting in to land at night, as was normal on such a voyage. Ambassadors from Mytilene supplied them with food and drink while they rowed and promised great rewards if they could make up the 24 hours start that the previous ship had on them. Eventually they reached Mytilene just as Paches was reading the orders delivered by the first ship. The mass of the citizens were saved, but Mytilene was deprived of her fleet and much of her territory.

At about the same time the small garrison of Plataia finally succumbed to starvation and surrendered to the Spartans. They were treated very harshly on the insistence of their neighbours the Thebans. All of the 225 surviving men were subjected to a 'trial' by the Spartans, at which they were each asked: 'Have you done anything of benefit to the Lakedaimonians (i.e. the Spartans) and their allies in the current war?' As none of the defenders could answer yes to this question, the Spartans decided that they were justified in executing all of them. The 110 women who had stayed behind were sold as slaves.

Naval warfare

At sea the war was fought almost entirely between fleets of triremes. These were warships rowed by up to 170 oarsmen and manned by 30 or more sailors and soldiers. The number of rowers could be varied so that a trireme could carry enough troops to act as an assault ship for small forces, or it could be used to tow and escort troop carriers if a larger army needed to be transported. When fully crewed the ships were dangerous offensive weapons in themselves, each sporting a heavy bronze ram on its prow, which could damage an enemy vessel's hull if it impacted with enough force. Consequently the best naval tactics involved manoeuvring behind or to the side of an enemy ship and rowing hard enough to smash the ram against its hull and rupture it. Another, more dangerous, tactic was for the helmsman to steer close into the enemy on one side and break off their oars, having signalled his own rowers to ship their oars just before the vessels made contact. The triremes were lightweight vessels that did not easily sink when they were holed, but instead they would often remain afloat, or perhaps partially submerged, and they could be towed away by whichever side was the victor. The crews of damaged ships were very vulnerable, however, and unless their own ships came quickly to their rescue they might be captured, or if the ship was completely awash with water they could easily drown. Surprisingly few Greeks were strong swimmers, since they did not swim for pleasure. Even if there was an accessible coastline close by it might be held by enemy troops who could kill or capture those men who did make it ashore.

Athenian naval superiority

In 429 the Peloponnesians sent out a fleet under the command of the Spartan Knemon to challenge the Athenian squadron under the command of Phormio based at Naupaktos. This naval base was strategically located to intercept Peloponnesian fleets sailing to and from Corinth, the Northern Peloponnese and Eastern Boiotia. Phormio had only 20 ships, whereas Knemon had a total of 47, drawn from Corinth and Sikyon. Nevertheless Phormio attacked and succeeded in putting the Peloponnesians on the defensive. They formed most of their ships into a circle with the prows facing outwards, their aim being to prevent the Athenians from getting behind any of them. Five of the best ships were stationed in the centre of the circle to attack any Athenian vessel that managed to get inside the formation. Phormio's response to this tactic was to tell the commanders of his own ships to sail around the fringes of this circle, getting gradually closer to the Peloponnesians and forcing them to back in towards each other. Eventually, with the help of a strong early morning wind, the circle of ships became too tightly packed and were unable to maintain their formation without colliding with each other. When it was clear that the Peloponnesians had lost all semblance of order Phormio attacked, sinking several of the enemy and capturing 12 ships.

The superior seamanship and tactics of the Athenians were rewarded with another success soon afterwards when a larger force of 77 Peloponnesian ships drove Phormio into the narrow stretch of water at Rhion, hoping to trap them against the northern shoreline, thus negating the greater speed and

manoeuvrability of the Athenians. After initially losing nine ships to this overwhelming force, Phormio and his remaining commanders broke away and retreated towards Naupaktos. The Peloponnesians pursued, but their lead ships became too spread out to support each other. As the final Athenian ship reached Naupaktos it went behind a merchant ship at anchor in the bay and turned on the foremost of the pursuing vessels, ramming it amidships and causing the rest to stop rowing and wait for their comrades. This decision left them sitting in the water and vulnerable to the swift counter-attacks of the Athenians, who now rowed out and rejoined the battle. Because they were now very close to the shore some of the Peloponnesians ran aground, or came close enough for the Messenians who were based at Naupaktos to swim out, some in their armour and swarm aboard some of the ships. The Athenians recaptured most of their own ships, which the Peloponnesians had been towing behind them. They also took six Peloponnesian vessels, on one of which was a Spartan commander called Timokrates, who killed himself rather than be captured by the Athenians. From this point onwards the Peloponnesians generally avoided naval confrontations with the Athenians until the Athenian navy had been seriously weakened by the Sicilian Expedition. In 425, when the Peloponnesian fleet sent to Corcyra was recalled to assist in removing Demosthenes' forces from Pylos, they chose to drag their ships over the narrow isthmus of Leukas rather than risk a meeting with the Athenian fleet, which was heading for Corcyra.

Nevertheless the Athenians did not have things entirely their own way at sea. In 429 the Spartans with Knemon were invited by the Megarians to transfer their surviving crews to 40 ships docked at Niasia, the Megarian port nearest to Athens. These ships could then be used to make a surprise attack on the Athenian port of Peiraieus, which was not well guarded. Strong winds and, in Thucydides' view, a lack of courage, caused them to abandon the idea of attacking Peiraieus and to strike at the island of

A sketch showing how the Athenian harbour at Mounychia in Peiraieus may have looked in the fourth century. Early on in the Peloponnesian War a daring attempt by the Spartans to attack the harbour showed the Athenians that they needed to fortify it. The entrance is narrow and there is a chain stretched across it to prevent unauthorised ships from getting in. (J F Coates)

Salamis instead. They captured three Athenian ships on the north of the island and did a considerable amount of damage before the arrival of an Athenian fleet and concerns over the state of their ships forced them to withdraw. The episode had demonstrated that Athenian territory was also vulnerable to seaborne attack and steps were taken to close off the harbour entrances at Peiraieus and station more ships on guard duty in the future.

Spartan defeat at Pylos

In the spring of 425 the Peloponnesian army, led by the young Spartan king Agis, again invaded Attika. They settled down to spend the summer devastating as much Athenian territory as possible and to try, once more, to force the Athenians into a major confrontation on land. Meanwhile, the Athenian generals Eurymedon and Sophokles were taking 40 ships to Sicily, via Corcyra. They made a detour into the area of Pylos on the western coast of the Peloponnese to attempt a scheme devised by the general-elect Demosthenes who was travelling with them.

Demosthenes' plan was to turn Pylos into a fortified post for a detachment of the Messenian exiles from Naupaktos to use as a base for conducting raids against Peloponnesian territory. From Pylos they could easily penetrate Messenia and, with their ability to speak the local dialect, their knowledge of the land and their kinship with the Messenians, they could stir up trouble for the Spartans in their own back yard. Demosthenes seems to have had some difficulty convincing the two current generals to carry out his plan, but eventually an improvised set of fortifications was built and Demosthenes was left there with five ships while the rest of the fleet sailed on towards Corcyra.

Initially the Spartans, did not see any serious threat from this Athenian foothold on their territory, but when King Agis and his advisers heard the news they abandoned

This bronze hoplite's helmet is in the style known as Corinthian. Such helmets afforded good protection to the wearer, but they severely restricted vision and hearing, making the hoplites heavily dependent on the coherence of their formation. This example is inscribed with the name Dendas, perhaps the person who dedicated it in a sanctuary. Many men preferred simpler helmets such as those seen in the illustration on page 86. (Ancient Art and Architecture)

their invasion of Attika and hurried to Pylos, gathering forces for a strike against Demosthenes. A Peloponnesian fleet that had been on its way to Corcyra was recalled to assist them. Demosthenes also sent for help and the Athenian fleet turned round at Zakynthos and headed back to Pylos.

This fifth-century sculpture from the temple of Aphaia on Aigina shows the hero Herakles, recognisable by his lionskin headress. He is in the act of shooting an arrow from a kneeling position. Archers were often carried on warships and would target the officers, steersmen, sailors and soldiers on enemy ships. (Ancient Art and Architecture)

The Spartans were determined to remove the enemy before their reinforcements could arrive. They attacked the Athenian position from the land and the sea for two days. They landed a small force of hoplites on the island of Sphakteria as part of the attempt to blockade the fort by land and sea. The Spartans were wary of the advantage that the Athenians had over them in naval confrontations, and seem to have decided that occupying the island would restrict Athenian access to the bay behind and prevent them from putting forces in the rear of the Spartans' own positions on land. Demosthenes beached his few remaining ships and deployed their crews as makeshift infantry. He and his men held out resolutely against almost continuous Spartan attacks. The Spartans' efforts took on a frantic edge, with one of their trireme commanders, Brasidas, putting his ship and his own life at risk by running his ship aground inside the area fortified by the Athenians and trying to force his way onto the land. He was badly wounded and lost his shield, but his bravery earned him much praise. The next day the Athenian fleet arrived, now numbering 50 vessels with the addition of ships from Naupaktos and four allied triremes from Chios.

The character of the confrontation changed dramatically once the Athenians had a strong naval force at their disposal. They easily drove the 43 Spartan ships away from the promontory of Pylos and onto the beaches in the bay, disabling some and capturing others. The blockade of the fort was lifted and the Spartans were left camped on the mainland watching helplessly as the Athenians sailed around Sphakteria unopposed. The most unfortunate result of this reversal of fortune was that 420 Peloponnesian hoplites and their Helot attendants were left stranded on the island.

The Spartans immediately sent a delegation from the *gerousia* and the ephorate to assess the situation. Their appraisal was an honest but bleak one. The situation was untenable for the men on Sphakteria because they could not be rescued and the Athenians could put their own soldiers on the island and eventually overwhelm them with sheer numbers. Even that might not be necessary, however, as there was virtually no food on the island, so they might easily be starved into surrender. The official delegation went straight to the Athenians and negotiated a truce, which allowed them to get provisions to their men and halted Athenian attacks. In return the Spartans surrendered what remained of their fleet and all the other triremes that they had back in Lakonia (a total of 60 ships), and sent an embassy to Athens to discuss a full peace treaty.

These negotiations could have ended the war, but instead they came to nothing. The Spartan envoys were prepared to make huge concessions to recover their men, but they refused to do so in front of a full session of the Athenian Assembly, which was what the Athenians insisted upon. Such a public display of weakness and humility was simply too much for the proud Spartans, accustomed as they were to having their most important decisions settled by a small group of senior citizens in a private meeting. There was a substantial body of opinion in Athens that favoured coming to terms now, but the more belligerent and arrogant feelings of Kleon and his supporters carried the day. When Kleon accused them of lacking sincerity the Spartans gave up and returned home. The truce was over and the Spartans requested the return of their ships, but the Athenians held on to them claiming that some of the details of the agreement had not been adhered to by the Spartans. Thus they were able to bring an end to Spartan naval activity for the time being and increase the pressure on the men trapped on Sphakteria.

More Athenian forces came to Pylos and a stalemate ensued. The conditions for the Athenians were not easy, as despite being masters of the sea, they did not control much of the coastline. Their fort was still under attack from the Spartan army on the mainland and Demosthenes had less than 1,000 soldiers to defend it. The Spartans offered cash rewards to anyone who was prepared to dodge the Athenian triremes patrolling around the island and bring food to the men there, either by swimming or in small boats. Enough Helots and Messenian fishermen volunteered to maintain the food supply. Eventually the Athenians began to feel the difficulty of supplying their own forces at such a great distance and in a confined space with nowhere to beach their ships in safety.

Back in Athens, Kleon's arrogant handling of the Spartan peace envoys put the onus on him to find a solution. He tried to deflect it by blaming the lack of progress on the board of generals. They should make a determined assault on the island and kill or capture the men there, he said. He would have done so already, if he were a general. One of the current generals, Nikias, took him at his word and invited him to select whatever forces he required and show them how to do it. The mass of citizens cheered this suggestion and shouted for Kleon to take up the challenge. Kleon was trapped by the kind of crowd-pleasing rhetoric that he normally used against others. He obtained a mixed force of tough, experienced hoplites from the Athenian citizen colonies of Lemnos and Imbros, and plenty of light infantry, both peltasts (light infantryman armed with javelins) and archers. He promised to destroy or capture the Spartans in 20 days.

The most amazing thing

Kleon's boast that he could resolve the situation in 20 days, coming from a man who had never previously held any military command, was probably a piece of sheer arrogance. However, he did have enough

This photo shows the bronze covering of a hoplite shield; the wooden core has long perished. It is pierced with letters that tell us it was booty taken from the Spartans at Pylos in 425 by the Athenians. The taking and dedicating of trophies was a key part of Greek warfare. They served as physical reminders of a god-given victory over the enemy. (American School of Classical Studies at Athens: Agora Excavations)

understanding of warfare to choose Demosthenes, the energetic commander whose plan had started the whole affair, as his chief adviser. Between them they came up with a tactically sound approach. They landed 800 hoplites on the island from both sides at dawn and caught the weary Spartan sentries completely by surprise. Once bridgeheads were established they flooded the island with the Messenians from the fort at Pylos, plus archers, peltasts and several thousand ordinary rowers from the fleet, whose only offensive weapons were sling stones and rocks. By holding the hoplites back from a direct engagement with the superior Spartan troops, and using the rest of his force to harry the enemy with missiles Demosthenes forced the Spartans to retreat rather than be gradually picked off where they stood. If they could have achieved close-quarter combat with the enemy the

Spartans might have been able to defeat them, but their heavy armour slowed them down. It also proved insufficient protection against the showers of arrows, javelins and stones from unarmoured men who easily ran off before they could be engaged by the lumbering hoplites. The Spartan commander, Epitadas, was driven back to an old fort on some high ground at the north end of the island where his surviving men, many of them severely wounded, prepared to make a stand. The Messenians, however, clambered over the cliffs and came up behind the Spartans, who were now surrounded and hopelessly outnumbered.

Before all the Spartans were killed Kleon and Demosthenes decided to offer them a chance to surrender. Epitadas was dead by this time, and his second in command was too badly wounded to move, so the third in command, Styphon, asked permission to consult his superiors among the Spartans on the mainland. A tense exchange of messages followed between Styphon and the dismayed Spartan officers across the bay. Finally the following instruction was issued: 'The Lakedaimonians (i.e. the Spartans) order you to do whatever you think is in your own best interests, provided you do not act dishonourably.' This remarkably unhelpful message was the final straw for the 292 men who were still alive. After a brief discussion they laid down their arms and surrendered to the Athenians. One hundred and twenty of them were full Spartan citizens.

'To the rest of the Greeks the most amazing thing that occurred in the whole of the war,' was how Thucydides chose to describe the Spartan surrender at Sphakteria. It was unthinkable that a Spartan force, however hard pressed, would give in to their opponents. They were expected to fight to the death, as King Leonidas and his 300 Spartans had chosen to do against the might of the Persian army at the battle of Thermopylai in 480. The blow to Spartan prestige was tremendous, and the boost to Athenian morale was equally great. The captured men were taken back to Athens by the fleet. A series of Spartan embassies tried to negotiate

their release, but the Athenians demanded more than they could give in return.

The strategic value of Demosthenes' plan was demonstrated because the Pylos fort now became a thorn in the side of the Spartans, as the Messenians, emboldened by their success on Sphakteria, launched raids into the surrounding countryside and caused many Helots to desert. Nikias and the other Athenian generals took a force of 80 ships and raided the territory of the Corinthians, doing considerable damage and establishing another fortified post at Methana, from where it was possible to ravage much of the Eastern Peloponnese.

Athens in the ascendancy

The following year, 424, the Athenians began to reap the benefits of having over 100 Spartan citizens as hostages. There was no Peloponnesian invasion of Attika this year because the Athenians had told the Spartans that they would execute the prisoners if this happened. On the contrary, it was the Athenians who took the initiative by attacking Kythera, a large island off the Peloponnesian coast to the south of Lakonia. The inhabitants were free men of Perioikoi status and their loyalty to the Spartans was guaranteed by their proximity to Lakonia and the Spartan practice of posting a garrison there with a Spartan commander. Nikias, Nikeratos and Autokles sailed there with 60 ships and an invasion force of 2,000 hoplites. They defeated the Kytherans and their garrison in a brief battle and persuaded them to swap sides, having already made them aware through messages from Nikias that their lives would be spared and they would be allowed to remain on the island if they gave in quickly. Kythera became another tribute-paying island in the Athenian Empire. From here it was easy for the Athenians to raid the coast of Lakonia, rendered especially vulnerable by the Spartans' rash decision to surrender their ships as part of the truce negotiated at Pylos. It was now the Spartans' turn to post cavalry

The scene on this Athenian red-figure wine jug shows Nike, the goddess who personified Victory, decorating a bronze tripod with a ribbon. Nike was usually portrayed with wings because the Greeks believed that it was the gods who told her whose side to fly to and no men could force her to stay with them.(Ashmolean Museum)

detachments and scatter small units of troops to defend their farmland from enemy attacks.

Nikias and his fellow generals took their fleet on to the eastern coast of the Peloponnese and attacked Thyrea, on the border between Argos and Lakonia. This was where the Spartans had settled refugees from Aigina. The local Spartan garrison, fearing a repeat of the Sphakteria episode, fled and left the hopelessly outnumbered Aiginetan exiles to the mercy of the Athenians. The Athenians killed many of them on the spot and transported the rest back to Athens for public execution. In this respect they

The small temple on the Acropolis dedicated to Athena Nike (Victory) was built in the 420s. It may reflect the Athenians' sense of triumph over their Peloponnesian enemies, but it was mostly decorated with scupltures showing mythological scenes or depicting the famous Athenian victory over the Persians in 490. (Ancient Art and Architecture)

behaved no better than the Thebans and Spartans had done towards the unfortunate citizens of Plataia.

The next Athenian target was Megara, where a pro-Athenian democratic faction in the city was plotting with Demosthenes to let an Athenian army into the city at dawn to force the Peloponnesian garrison to surrender. The plot was only partially successful but it did enable the large Athenian army to take control of the nearby port of Nisaia. The garrison of Peloponnesian troops stationed there offered to pay a ransom for themselves and hand over the Spartans among them in return for safe passage. This was doubtless another symptom of the low esteem in which the Spartans were held after the Sphakteria débâcle. The city of Megara itself was not captured, however, partly thanks to the resolute action taken by the Spartan Brasidas, who was at Sikyon recruiting troops for an expedition into the Thracian region. He quickly assembled a force of 4,000 hoplites who linked up with some Boiotian cavalry to check the Athenian advance on the city. The hoplite force that Brasidas used was largely composed of Corinthians, whose territory bordered Megara and who were likely to suffer the most from further Athenian gains in the area. At this point in his narration of the events of the war Thucydides makes the following comment on the Athenian citizens' ambition and overconfidence:

So completely were they taken in by their current good fortune that they assumed that no-one could possibly stand against them; and they believed that both the possible and the impossible alike could be accomplished, regardless of whether their resources were great or meagre. The reason for this was the completely unlooked for success in whatever they did, which greatly raised their expectations.

Athenian defeat at Delion

The Athenians were content to retain the port of Nisaia and turned their attention to the Boiotians, their neighbours to the north of Attika, who were dominated by the city of Thebes, Sparta's principal ally outside of the Peloponnese. Demosthenes and his fellow general Hippokrates had devised a complex plan to capture and fortify Delion, a position on the coast of Boiotia, near Tanagra. From there they hoped to force most of the Boiotians to revolt against Theban control. The plan called for two armies to converge on Delion from the north and south. Demosthenes' army was to include allies from Akarnania in Western Greece, some Phokians and Boiotians from Orchomenos, while Hippokrates led an army composed largely of Athenian citizens. The plan went wrong from the outset. Demosthenes' intentions were betrayed to the Thebans and he was prevented from making the rendezvous. Hippokrates and the Athenian hoplites reached Delion and fortified it, but as they were heading back to Attika they were confronted by the Thebans and most of the other Boiotians. As often happened in a hoplite battle the right wing of each army drove back its opponents, but the superior Boiotian cavalry forces scattered the Athenian right wing and the heavy concentration of Theban hoplites forced the Athenian left into headlong flight. Over 1,000 Athenians were killed, including their general Hippokrates.

Brasidas fights back

In 424 the Spartans decided to strike at a vulnerable area of the Athenian Empire, the Greek cities of the north-eastern Aegean, especially the peninsula of Chalkidike. Unable to mount any naval expeditions, they sent a small army overland from the Peloponnese to Northern Greece. It was under the command of Brasidas, the Spartan who had fought so bravely at Pylos and was beginning to gain a reputation as a skilful tactician. The Spartans were not prepared to risk more of their own citizens so far from home, so his force consisted of 1,000 hoplite mercenaries, from various parts of the

This photo is of the Hellenic naval vessel *Olympias*, a working reconstruction of an Athenian trireme. Such warships routinely used their sails for long voyages, but they were propelled by their oars alone during battles; the masts were removed and stored on land. Some triremes were used to transport soldiers and a few were even converted to carry up to 30 horses. (Ancient Art and Architecture)

Peloponnese and 700 Helots who had volunteered to fight as hoplites in exchange for their freedom. Funding came from the king of Macedon and the recently formed League of the Greek cities of Chalkidike, all of whom wanted to reduce Athenian influence in the area.

One of Brasidas' first successes was against the city of Amphipolis. He had already persuaded the Chalkidian cities of Akanthos and Stageira to revolt from Athens, but Amphipolis was a more difficult, though tempting target. It had been founded under Athenian direction in 437/436 to control a strategically vital crossing point of the river Strymon, a major trade and communication route, and to provide a base for exploitation of the natural resources of the Pangeion mountain region, principally timber for ship-building,

silver and gold. It had a population drawn from all parts of Greece, with only a small Athenian element. The strength of these citizens' loyalties to the Athenians was dubious, but there was an Athenian hoplite garrison there, commanded by the general Eukles.

The sudden appearance of Brasidas, accompanied by Chalkidian forces from the cities that had joined him, caught the inhabitants of Amphipolis completely unprepared. Many of them were outside the city walls, working on their farmland. Nevertheless Eukles managed to despatch a ship to alert the historian Thucydides, who was an Athenian general for this year and had a force of seven triremes on the island of Thasos, less than a day's sail away to the south east.

The news of Brasidas' arrival was communicated to Thucydides as quickly as possible. The distance between Amphipolis and Thasos is about 50 miles (80km) and the journey would normally have been a relatively straightforward one for experienced mariners. It was winter however, and navigating across to the mainland, along the coast and up the river Strymon in poor weather and failing light could have been quite hazardous. Thucydides does not say how difficult his voyage was, but his failure to cover the distance in less than six hours is certainly not indicative of incompetence or hesitancy. He says that he set out 'immediately' and 'at full speed' with his seven ships from Thasos, but he still failed to reach the city in time to prevent its surrender, and nearly failed to save the city of Eion, further down the river Strymon.

Thucydides says that even the Athenians in Amphipolis did not expect relieving forces to arrive quickly, which suggests that they were uncertain when, or possibly whether, their call for help would reach him, in spite of the fact that he was close by. Perhaps there was an additional worry about what his reaction to the news would be? They would only know if he had heeded their call when they saw his ships coming up the river from Eion. Yet Brasidas decided to offer them generous, remarkably un-Spartan surrender terms, allowing the inhabitants to retain their possessions and political rights in exchange for acknowledging Spartan authority. Those who did not wish to stay under these terms were allowed to take their possessions and leave unmolested. In contrast, when the Plataians finally surrendered in 427 all of the men, except those who could claim that they had been helping the Spartans, were killed and the women who had stayed with them were enslaved. Unlike many other Spartan commanders during the war, Brasidas was operating a long way from home and had no-one overseeing his actions, but his leniency to the inhabitants was based on his own expectation that a relief force would arrive quickly and that Thucydides would easily be able to exploit his local connections to summon up further forces to challenge Brasidas.

So why did Eukles and his compatriots not come to the same conclusion and determine to hold out even for a single day? Thucydides says that the population of Amphipolis felt they were better off surrendering on Brasidas, 'generous terms' and they would not listen to the Athenian commander. It would seem that a lack of firm information on the prospects of relief, combined with the certainty of lenient treatment by Brasidas, caused a catastrophic loss of confidence in the Athenians. It was easier to believe in the visible Spartan forces than in the unseen fleet of Thucydides whose approach could only be presumed to be happening. Without any means of communicating quickly with each other over long distances, Greek commanders were constantly plagued by doubts and fears of betrayal and abandonment. Brasidas was able to exploit this weakness to seize control of a vital Athenian outpost. The consequence for Thucydides was that the Athenian Assembly chose to blame him for the loss of Amphipolis and he was exiled from his home city. His loss was posterity's gain, however, as he was able to travel around the Greek world gathering vital information for his history of the Peloponnesian War.

The fragile truce of 423

Brasidas continued to campaign in the area, but he met some determined resistance from the local Athenian garrison in the city of Torone, until some of its population opened the gates and the Athenians were forced to flee by ship. Emboldened by his successes he put the resources of Amphipolis to good use by building triremes on the banks of the river Strymon.

The Athenians clearly had to find a way to put a stop to what Brasidas was doing and their possession of the Spartans taken at Pylos in 425 gave them a strong bargaining position in peace negotiations. Sparta persuaded her allies to agree to offer a truce for one year as a preliminary step towards a long-term settlement. The Athenian assembly accepted and oaths were taken by representatives of both sides in the summer of 423. The terms of the truce included a clause allowing each side to keep its own territory, specific restrictions on movement of troops and communications with strategically sensitive areas, particularly around Megara, restrictions on Peloponnesian movement at sea and a ban on accepting any deserters from the other side, whether they were free men or slaves. This would have included any more Messenians fleeing to Pylos and should also have put a stop to the defections from Athens' tribute-paying cities in Northern Greece.

In the midst of the negotiations for this truce Skione, one of the Chalkidian cities, revolted. Brasidas, who had persuaded the Skionians to come over to his side, claimed that it was not contrary to the terms of the truce because it happened before the oaths were taken. The Athenians were furious with the Skionians, however, and Kleon persuaded the assembly to vote for a decree that the city should be sacked and its citizens executed as a punishment. This harsh decision did not deter Skione's neighbour Mende from changing sides as well, although in this case there was no doubt that it happened after the truce was ratified. Brasidas might have made even greater gains had he not had to divert most of his forces to a joint campaign with his royal ally and paymaster King Perdikkas of Macedon. The Athenians took advantage of his absence to send an expedition to the region under the generals Nikias and Nikostratos. They managed to recover Mende, whose citizens changed sides again in time to avoid the full wrath of Athenian retribution, but Skione held out longer. Brasidas might have been able to raise the siege there too, if Spartan reinforcements had managed to get through Thessaly, but they were blocked with the connivance of King Perdikkas, who had fallen out with Brasidas and was now co-operating with the Athenians.

Deaths of Kleon and Brasidas

The war continued in a sporadic fashion despite the truce. The Athenians tried to revive their interests in Sicily by encouraging opposition to Syracuse, but no significant progress was made. A Boiotian force captured, through treachery, the fort of Panakton on the border between Athens and Boiotia. This was not a serious defeat for the Athenians,

but it increased the vulnerability of Northern Attika to raids and made it more difficult for the Athenians to bring supplies into their city from the island of Euboia. In the meetings of the Assembly there was a growing sense of impatience, which led to demands for some decisive activity on the part of their generals. This sense of frustration made it easier for Kleon to persuade the Athenian assembly to vote for a strong expedition to be sent to the north to deal with Brasidas. The Assembly authorised Kleon to take command of 30 triremes, with 1,200 Athenian hoplites, 300 cavalry and a strong force drawn from the subject allies. He gathered further troops from those besieging Skione and attacked Torone. The city was quickly taken by a combined land and sea assault. The Toronian women and children were sold into slavery, while the surviving 700 men, consisting of some Toronians, some Chalkidians from other cities and a few Peloponnesians, were taken back to Athens to join the other enemy prisoners.

The main target for Kleon's expedition was the recovery of Amphipolis. Brasidas also realised the importance of the city and he hired additional Thracian mercenaries to bolster his defences. Kleon based himself at nearby Eion, but he took his army close enough to Amphipolis to observe the dispositions of Brasidas' forces inside the city. When they appeared to be preparing to come out for battle he ordered his men to withdraw. But Brasidas had selected 150 of his best hoplites as a strike force and he rushed out of the gates while Kleon was still trying to turn his army round and organise it for the march back to Eion. As more of Brasidas' men poured out of the city to engage them the Athenians panicked and fled. Kleon was killed by a Thracian mercenary along with about 600 hoplites. On the other side there were only seven casualties, but they included Brasidas, who had once again chosen to lead by example and was fatally wounded. He survived long enough to hear the extent of his victory and the jubilant citizens of Amphipolis gave him a magnificent funeral and installed a shrine

The Propylaia of the Athenian Acropolis was a monumental gateway to the sanctuary which contained temples altars and other sacred buildings. Ritual processions of men, women and children passed through it during the many religious festivals that were celebrated by the citizens in honour of their gods. (Ancient Art and Architecture)

to him as their honorary founder, in place of the original Athenian founder. When news of Brasidas' death was brought back home he was hailed as the best of the Spartans, but his mother is reputed to have said: 'My son Brasidas was indeed a fine man, nevertheless he was not as good as many other Spartans.' For this display of traditional Spartan reticence and patriotism the ephors decided to award her public honours.

The Peace of Nikias

The deaths of both Brasidas and Kleon took a lot of the momentum out of the war between Athens and Sparta. Both had been energetic and ambitious in proposing and carrying out schemes to wear down the other

side. Their simultaneous deaths were taken by everyone involved as symbolic of the stalemate that had been reached after nearly 10 years of war. Those who advocated peace were now able to push along negotiations for a long-term treaty. By the end of 422 the Spartans were faced with the prospect of further Helot revolts if the raids from Pylos and Kythera continued. More urgent, however was the need to recover over 100 full Spartan citizens from the Athenians. Why were these few Spartans who became trapped on Sphakteria so precious that their imminent capture brought the Spartan war effort to a standstill and securing their return dominated Spartan thinking for nearly four years? There were other, allied prisoners to be exchanged, of course, including those captured by Kleon at Torone. The Spartan manpower shortage referred to earlier must also be part of the explanation. In addition, Thucydides tells us that some of them were important people back in Sparta, with relations among the Spartan citizens who held high office, yet after their return they were condemned as cowards and deprived of their citizen rights for surrendering instead of fighting on. Ultimately it may have been the symbolic and emotional significance of these prisoners that made the Spartans desperate to wrest them from the grasp of the gloating Athenians. As long as they remained in Athens they were living, walking proof that, for all their training, discipline and haughty disregard for others, the Spartans were not the bravest and the best of the Greeks. Once they were back home they could be stripped of their Spartan status and replaced by some of the other, braver Spartans that Brasidas' mother had ranked above even her remarkable son.

For the Athenians there was also a growing manpower shortage, as the deployment of allied troops in Kleon's forces illustrates. They also would have welcomed the prospect of recovering prisoners held by Peloponnesians and their allies, and they were probably just as concerned about the heavy toll that the war effort was taking on their financial reserves and the revenues from their slightly diminished empire. The confidence that the Sphakteria victory had produced must have been severely dented by the defeats at Delion and Amphipolis. The Athenian general Nikias played a leading role in the negotiations that produced a peace treaty, so modern scholars have named the treaty after him.

It is clear that the aim was to conclude a treaty similar to the Thirty Years' Peace which had been negotiated in 446, but with an initial duration of 50 years. Each side was supposed to give up any territories that it had gained by force during the war, such as the border fortress of Panakton. The Thebans refused to restore Plataia and the Athenians insisted on holding onto the Megarian port of Niasia, both claiming that these places had surrendered voluntarily. The Athenians recovered the strategically vital city of Amphipolis, but the other Chalkidian cities were allowed to declare themselves autonomous, as long as they resumed their payments of tribute to Athens. The rebellious citizens of Skione were less fortunate. Their change of sides had so angered the

Athenians that, when they first heard of it, they were persuaded by Kleon to vote for a harsh punishment. The men were to be executed and the women and children sold into slavery. This time, unlike the situation over the revolt of Mytilene, there was no change of heart. Skione's stubborn resistance seems to have hardened the attitude of the Athenians, who were not prepared to be merciful towards subject allies who had tried to break away from their empire.

The Spartans' main requirements were met with the return of Pylos and Kythera to them and a general exchange of prisoners. They also concluded a new treaty with Athens that included a clause promising Athenian help in the case of another Helot revolt. Nevertheless, they could hardly claim that their grandiose mission to liberate the Greeks from the tyranny of Athens had been achieved. The Athenians and their empire were still there.

The peace of Nikias certainly did not last for 50 years. Within months of the Athenians and Spartans agreeing to cease hostilities and exchange conquests their relationship had deteriorated into mutual suspicion. Gradually the tension escalated as it had done in the 430s, until both sides were openly at war with each other again. Indeed, Thucydides, looking back on these events with the benefit of hindsight did not think it was a proper peace at all, but merely a break in open hostilities directed against the territory of the two protagonists. Outside of Attika and Lakonia, he argued, each side did much to harm the interests of the other until the renewal of the conflict was inevitable. In part the failure to maintain peace can be blamed on the reluctance of the allies on both sides to accept the terms of the treaty. The Corinthians and the Boiotians both refused to be bound by it, particularly as it was made without their consent and included a provision for alterations to be made by mutual agreement between Athens and Sparta, without reference to any allies. The Boiotians demonstrated their disapproval by holding on to Panakton until they had destroyed its fortifications.

Athenian irritation with what they saw as failure by the Spartans to keep their side of the agreement was exploited by an ambitious young politician called Alkibiades, a relative of Perikles. He persuaded the Assembly that the way to get back at the Spartans was to encourage trouble for them in the Peloponnese. An excellent opportunity to do just this came about because the peace treaty which had been concluded between Sparta and Argos in 451 was about to expire. Throughout the Archidamian War the Argives had maintained a neutral position to their own benefit. Unlike many of their neighbours they were not economically and socially worn out from 10 years of inconclusive warfare. The people of Argos were also very well aware of their former glories, celebrated in myths and stories of Argive kings leading the Greeks. A democratic faction in Argos started working with Alkibiades and his supporters in Athens to create a new, anti-Spartan coalition by recruiting cities like Elis and Mantinea who resented the extent of Spartan influence in the Peloponnese.

In 419 the Argives attacked Epidauros, in order to secure their eastern flank against the Corinthians and to provide a convenient landing point for Athenian forces, which could not enter the Peloponnese by land because the Corinthians blocked their route. The Spartans had to respond to this show of Argive force, so they reinforced Epidauros by sea. The Argives were dismayed that the Athenians, whose naval strength was far superior to the Spartans, did nothing to hinder this move. What the Athenians did decide to do was to add an additional section to the public inscription recording the terms of the Peace of Nikias, claiming that the Spartans did not keep their oaths. In 419 the Spartans gathered a substantial army in the Peloponnese to attack Argos, and summoned further troops from their more distant allies, including Corinth and Boiotia. The Argives marched into the heart of the Peloponnese to try to prevent these forces joining up, but they were unsuccessful. Dividing his forces, the Spartan king, Agis, manoeuvred the

Argives into a vulnerable position between a small Spartan-led force and a larger one comprising the Boiotians, Corinthians and other allies of Sparta. But instead of pressing on to what seemed like certain victory, Agis met with a few representatives of the Argives and, without consulting any of his allies, agreed to withdraw under a truce that was to last for four months.

Agis was severely criticised back in Sparta, but the pious and tradition-bound Spartans felt obliged to observe the truce. He was, however, obliged by the ephors to accept a 10-man board of special advisors to prevent him making any similar political errors. In 418 the Argives gathered their allies once more and set out to force other Peloponnesian states to join their coalition. They easily persuaded the city of Orchomenos to come over to them and moved south to Mantinea, intending to use the city as a base from which to put pressure on Tegea. The Spartans were forced to respond to a direct threat to one of their principal allies.

The battle of Mantinea

Led by Agis, the Spartan army marched into the territory of Mantinea and implemented their standard policy of ravaging the enemy's land in order to force them to come out and offer battle in defence of their crops. Unfortunately, in that part of the Peloponnese the harvest was mostly completed by this time, and the damage did not amount to much. The allies were not eager to risk a battle as they were hoping for reinforcements in the shape of a large force of about 3,000 hoplites from Elis and a further 1,000 from Athens. When they eventually did emerge from Mantinea, instead of marching directly against the Spartans they took up a defensive position on the slopes of the nearby hills and waited for Agis and the Spartans to make the next move.

Agis was determined to force a battle, so he ordered his army to advance towards the enemy, up an increasingly steep slope.

Thucydides says that when the two armies were close enough to throw javelins or cast stones at each other, one of the older men in the Spartan ranks called out to Agis, saying that he was trying to make up for one mistake with another. He meant that Agis was trying to atone for his earlier, ignominious withdrawal from Argos by leading a reckless attack on a strong enemy position. It may well be that the old man whose words brought Agis to his senses was one of the members of the *gerousia*, the Spartan council of elders; he may even have been one of the 10 advisers. Whatever its origin, the rebuke seems to have worked, as Agis ordered a last-minute about turn, taking the army back to the city of Tegea. He was fortunate that his foolhardy advance and sudden retreat confused the commanders of the Argive coalition. They did not immediately try to pursue the retreating Spartans, probably because they were concerned that their opponents might turn about once more and attack them when they were no longer in such a strong position.

King Agis and his allies were still faced with the problem of how to draw the coalition allies down from their commanding position and into a more favourable location to engage them in battle. They decided that as an alternative to threatening the Mantineans' crops, they would threaten their water supplies by diverting the course of the main river in the area so that, when the rains came in the autumn, it would flood the territory of the Mantineans and ruin their land. In order to prevent this the enemy would be forced to come down from the hills and onto the flood plains of the river, where the flat land would not give an advantage to either side. This idea must have been suggested by the Tegeans who had a long history of disputes with the Mantineans over how to manage the flood plains.

In the meantime the Argives and their allies were on the move. The senior commanders of this coalition force were members of the aristocracy of Argos, the

Thousand, whose relations with the Spartans had usually been good, but who were under pressure from their own citizens to demonstrate that they would not come to terms with the enemy in order to avoid a battle. They were also expected to fulfil on the promises offered by the new alliance to places like Mantinea, which were looking for a genuine alternative to the traditional dominance of Sparta in the Peloponnese. The Argives and their allies, therefore, moved down from the hilltop and onto the plain to the south of Mantinea. They lined up in the order of battle they had decided upon for the confrontations with the Spartans.

Their right wing, traditionally the strongest in a hoplite battle, was occupied by the Mantineans, whose home territory was now under threat, and by hoplites from some of the smaller cities of Arkadia. Next to them were the elite 1,000 hoplites from Argos, while the bulk of the Argive hoplites occupied the centre and the left wing, along with 1,000 hoplites and some cavalry from Athens.

Meanwhile the Spartans had advanced towards Mantinea, unaware that the opposing army had left its previous position and was now much closer to them. Emerging from a wood, they were surprised and disconcerted to find the enemy drawn up for battle in front of them. Agis hastily arranged his forces for the battle, adopting the usual Spartan procedure of putting the Skiritai, hoplites from the Skiris region of Arkadia, on his left wing, alongside hoplite companies formed from freed Helots, including those men who had returned from Brasidas' expedition to Thrace. At the centre were the Lakonian hoplites, both Spartans and Perioikoi. The Spartans' other Arkadian allies, including the Tegeans, were stationed on the right wing, with some Spartan officers to stiffen their resolve. At the extreme ends of each wing Agis stationed a couple of hundred Spartan cavalry. Both sides had some cavalry and a small number of light-armed troops, armed with bows, javelins and slings, but the bulk of each army consisted of hoplites, 8,000 on the Argive side and about 9,000 on the Spartan side. These were very large numbers for a hoplite confrontation and the ensuing battle demonstrated several of the key strengths and weaknesses of this form of massed infantry warfare.

Thucydides observes that there is a marked tendency for a hoplite phalanx to move to its right as it approaches the enemy. This is the result of the fact that each man's right side feels vulnerable because his shield cannot fully cover that side of his body. To compensate he moves closer to the protruding shield of the man on his right, and so on down the line, resulting in a general drift to the right of the whole army. So, as both armies advanced, each one began to extend its right wing beyond the opponents' corresponding left wing. At the battle of Mantinea this tendency was exaggerated by the fact that the Spartan army was larger and its front was wider, so that the line of the Tegeans and Spartans on Agis' left extended well beyond that of the Athenians and Argives opposite them. Conversely, on Agis' left wing the line of the Skiritai and freed Helots did not extend as far as the line of the Mantineans.

Worried that his left would be outflanked and easily defeated, Agis ordered the men there to move towards their left. However, this threatened to open up a significant gap in the line, so, as the two armies closed with each other Agis told two Spartan company commanders to take their men from the right of the Spartan hoplite line and fill the developing gap between his left wing and centre. They refused, being experienced Spartan officers who understood that to do so would leave an even more dangerous gap between the right wing and the centre. Agis tried to get his left wing to move to the right again, to close up the front line of his army, but it was too late and as the armies clashed there was a considerable gap between the freed Helots and the Spartans.

This relief sculpture comes from a large tomb built for a local aristocrat in South Western Asia Minor around 400. It shows hoplites fighting in a phalanx formation. If the discipline and cohesion of the formation was maintained it was very difficult to overcome. An unexpected attack, or one coming from the flank or rear, could easily panic the hoplites and break up their formation. (Ancient Art and Architecture)

The battle of Mantinea 418 BC

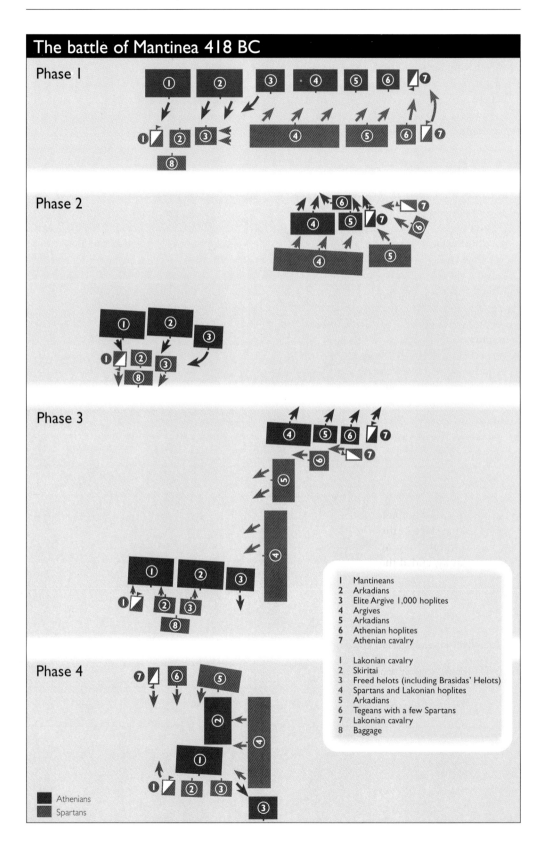

Phase 1

Phase 2

Phase 3

1 Mantineans
2 Arkadians
3 Elite Argive 1,000 hoplites
4 Argives
5 Arkadians
6 Athenian hoplites
7 Athenian cavalry

1 Lakonian cavalry
2 Skiritai
3 Freed helots (including Brasidas' Helots)
4 Spartans and Lakonian hoplites
5 Arkadians
6 Tegeans with a few Spartans
7 Lakonian cavalry
8 Baggage

Phase 4

Athenians
Spartans

The Mantineans, their Arkadian allies and the 1,000 Argives exploited this gap, driving Agis' left wing back and nearly encircling it. If they had slowed down, consolidated the split between the two parts of Agis' army and then moved to their left, attacking the main formation of Spartan hoplites from the flank and rear, they might have won a remarkable victory. Instead they rushed forward, breaking up Agis' left wing and driving the men before them until they reached the baggage train, which was guarded by a few older men, many of whom they killed. Meanwhile, their own centre and left wing were faring badly. The Spartans easily overcame the Argives in front of them, who panicked and fled after only a brief show of resistance. They were older men, less well trained than the 1,000 elite hoplites who were pursuing Agis' defeated right wing, and more accustomed to fear the Spartans. The Athenians on the extreme left of the Argive army were being encircled. It was only the brave action of their cavalry that prevented a complete rout. So the battle had become divided into two separate groups of victorious hoplites pursuing their defeated and demoralised enemies. Such circumstances were typical of hoplite confrontations and, as was often the case, it was the army which retained the most discipline and cohesion after the initial stage of the engagement that was able to win the day. Agis, seeing his left wing in disarray, ended the pursuit of the

enemy centre and left so that he could turn the bulk of his army against the Mantineans, Arkadians and elite Argives, encircling them and inflicting heavy casualties.

Once again, however, an experienced senior Spartan officer intervened. This was Pharax, one of the men appointed to advise Agis after his last campaign against Argos. Pharax drew King Agis away from the front line where he was fighting and told him to give orders to leave an escape route for the 1,000 elite Argive hoplites. The historian Diodoros says that this was because they were so determined and desperate that they might have inflicted serious damage on the Spartan forces, but it may well be that there was a political angle to Pharax's advice. The elite Argive hoplites were men from the richest families in Argos and they were those most likely to support an oligarchic regime, which was what the Spartans wanted. If they were slain, however, their influence would have been lost and the pro-Athenian, democratic element in Argos would have found it easier to continue governing and pursuing its anti-Spartan alliances. It was, therefore, the Mantineans, the ordinary Argives, the Athenians and the Arkadians who suffered the most casualties at the hands of the Spartans, losing over 1,000 men between them, while the elite Argives got away almost unscathed.

The immediate consequence of this victory was the restoration of the Spartans' military reputation, but it did not produce a long-term resolution of the conflicts between the Greek states. Reluctant allies of Sparta also knew what to expect if they looked elsewhere for support. They had defeated the rival city of Argos, bringing a halt to her scheme to dominate the Peloponnese in place of Sparta. The following year the oligarchic faction in Argos was able to overthrow the democratic government with Spartan assistance. A democratic revival followed soon after, however, while the Spartans were busy with one of their many religious festivals, and the oligarchic regime was removed. New overtures were made to the Athenians and there were further plans for joint operations in the

1. As the two armies approached Agis ordered the men on his left wing to move to their left. The Spartans who were told to fill the gap between his left and centre did not do so. Both armies drifted to their right as they came closer.
2. The Mantineans, Arkadians and elite Argive 1,000 drove the left wing of Agis' army back towards their baggage. The Spartan centre and right defeated and panicked the Argives, Arkadians and Athenians in front of them.
3. Agis turned the soldiers on his right and centre to help his stricken left wing. Before the elite Argive 1,000 were surrounded Pharax advised Agis to leave them an escape route.
4. As the elite Argive 1,000 escaped the Spartans surrounded the remaining Mantinean and Arkadian hoplites, inflicting heavy casualties.

Peloponnese. The Athenians, meanwhile, were re-establishing a healthy financial position. Peace with Sparta made it easier to draw in revenues from trade and the tribute of their allies, while at the same time it reduced expenditure on military pay and equipment. In 416 they launched an expedition to take control of the small island of Melos, whose population might have hoped for assistance from the Spartans, but who were abandoned to the less than tender mercy of the Athenians.

Athens and Sicily

In the spring of 415 an embassy arrived at Athens from her ally Egesta, one of the smaller cities of Sicily, located in the North Western part of the island. Athens' alliance with Egesta dated back to the 450s when the Athenians were looking for opportunities to make alliances with enemies of the Spartans and their allies. They had also made alliances with the Sicilian Greeks of Rhegion and Leontini around this time and they had intervened in Leontini's struggle with Syracuse in 427, to counter the potential for Syracuse and her Sicilian allies to send assistance to the Peloponnesians. Syracuse had been founded by settlers from Corinth, and it would have been natural for the Syracusans to join the line up alongside their mother city against the Athenians.

The Egestans were seeking help against their southern neighbour Selinous, an ally of Syracuse. Realising that the Athenians would not send significant help if there were no funds available to pay for it, the Egestans insisted that they would be able to cover most of the expenses of a large fleet and army. Initial Athenian interest was tempered by the need to have proof of the availability of the funds, so an investigative embassy was despatched to Egesta. They returned bearing 60 talents of silver with them and the promise that there was plenty more where that came from because the Sicilians were very wealthy. In fact they had been fooled by the Egestans who invited the envoys to dine in a different

house each night and plied them with rich food and plenty of wine, served in expensive gold and silver dishes and cups. What the overindulging Athenian envoys had failed to notice, however, was that the same silver and gold utensils were being used on each occasion, so the impression of a highly prosperous city with riches was all a clever ruse.

Having heard this news of an apparent abundance of money to finance an expedition to Sicily the citizens of Athens debated what proportion of their own men and materials to commit to it. The Athenian forces that had operated in Sicily in the years 427–424, ostensibly on behalf of Leontini, had made some headway in securing allies, obtaining funds and using their limited military resources to thwart the imperial ambitions of Syracuse and prevent any assistance coming from Sicily to the Peloponnesians. It is likely that Alkibiades and his ambitious supporters played on renewed fears of Syracusan intervention in the war, but at the same time they invited the Athenians to revive their dream of conquering Sicily and helping themselves to the wealth and resources of the Western Mediterranean. They painted a picture of weak opponents, so divided by internal strife that they could not possibly resist the military might of Athens. Most of the Athenians had no idea how large the cities of Sicily were, or how strong and determined their citizens might be. Alkibiades played on this ignorance to make the success of the expedition seem almost inevitable. The older, more cautious leaders like Nikias advocated rejecting the request altogether and concentrating on problems closer to home, especially the recovery of the coastal regions of Thrace. This objective, they argued, was more realistic and more important than a wild adventure into the West.

The ambitious, imperialist argument prevailed, however, and the assembly voted to send 60 ships under the joint command of three generals, Alkibiades, Nikias and a veteran commander called Lamachos. The official tasks of the generals were to help Egesta against Selinous and to re-establish the city of Leontini, which had been broken up by

Syracuse in 424. There was also a third, very vague directive given to the generals: 'If the war were to be going well for them, they were also to manage matters in Sicily in whatever manner they might feel was in the best interests of the Athenians'. Thucydides was in no doubt that this meant that the real intention of the expedition was to conquer Sicily. He was sure that the lure of fabulous wealth and limitless conquests had won out over Nikias' warnings against overambition. When Nikias tried to dissuade the assembly by insisting that the forces allocated were too small and that a huge, expensive commitment was needed to bring about success, he expected the citizens to have second thoughts. Instead they voted to allow the generals to take as large a force as they thought fit.

Shortly before the expedition set sail an ominous act of religious vandalism occurred. All over Athens, at cross-roads, public sanctuaries and outside the entrances to many private houses there were statues called herms. They usually consisted of marble blocks surmounted by busts of the god of travellers, Hermes, often with ithyphallic appendages. One night a group of men went round the city systematically mutilating these statues. The timing and scale of the damage clearly implied an orchestrated attempt to create an omen that would cause a delay or even cancel the expedition. A general call for information about the apparent conspiracy produced no immediate suspects, but accusations were brought against several wealthy citizens, including Alkibiades, of religious sacrilege. They were accused of conducting obscene parodies of the Sacred Mysteries, archaic fertility rituals celebrated twice each year by initiates in the cult of the goddess Demeter and her daughter Persephone at Eleusis, near the border with Megara. Alkibiades demanded an immediate trial, but it was decided to allow the expedition to sail while further enquiries were carried out. A series of dubious denunciations and confessions followed, some concerned with parodies of the Mysteries and others the equally mysterious mutilation of the herms. The ordinary Athenian citizens suspected,

without much clear evidence, that a group of the wealthiest citizens were hatching a plot to overthrow the democracy and install an oligarchic government. Several individuals fled the city and it was eventually decided to recall Alkibiades to stand trial.

When the expedition reached Athens' ally of Rhegion, on the toe of Italy, they were denied entry to the city, but a market was set up and they drew their fleet out of the water and onto the beach. Three ships were sent off to Egesta and they returned with the bad news that there was no more money available from that particular source. The people of Rhegion, despite their Ionian kinship with Leontini, refused to join in the war and declared their neutrality. The three Athenian generals considered their options, but they disagreed on how to proceed. Nikias suggested sailing round to Egesta on the western side of Sicily to try to obtain further funds. With or without this money they could settle the dispute between Egesta and Selinous, by force if necessary, and then come back around the southern coastline, allowing the cities a good view of the powerful Athenian fleet. If an opportunity should present itself they might also sort out the quarrel between Leontini and Syracuse. Alkibiades was in favour of delaying any offensive action until they had gathered more allies among the Sicilians, both the native population and the Greek cities. Lamachos' proposal was the simplest, an immediate direct assault on Syracuse, before the enemy had made adequate preparations. He argued that the Syracusans' lack of readiness, combined with the fear induced by the appearance of such a large Athenian force would give them their best chance for a quick victory.

Eventually Lamachos was persuaded to agree to Alkibiades' plan and so Nikias was outvoted two to one. The Athenians set off to persuade more of the Greek cities of eastern Sicily to side with them. At Messene they were not allowed into the city, but Naxos agreed to join their alliance and Katana was won over. Soon after the success at Katana, however, a trireme arrived from Athens with a summons for Alkibiades and several others to return to stand trial for their parts in the

Sicily during the Peloponnesian War

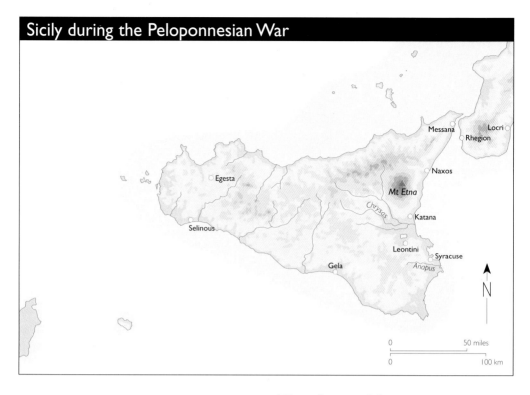

scandalous parodying of the Eleusinian Mysteries. Alkibiades was reluctant to go back, fearing, with some justification, that his political opponents in Athens had been conspiring against him in his absence and that he could not expect a fair trial because of the atmosphere of panic and suspicion that had been created back in Athens. When they reached Thurii in Southern Italy he escaped and eventually made his way to Sparta, where he was given a cautious welcome. He was condemned in his absence and sentenced to death, as were several others.

Nikias and Lamachos attempted to press on with the campaign in Sicily, raising some funds and making a sudden attack on Syracuse, which resulted in a defeat for the Syracusans outside their city. The battle indicated that the Athenian forces needed cavalry support and more money to wage a successful war against Syracuse and because it was getting late in the year the two Athenian generals decided to abandon military action and retire to Katana for the winter.

The siege of Syracuse

In the spring of 414 the Athenians moved on to the offensive and attacked Syracuse in earnest. They brought 250 cavalrymen from Athens and 300 talents of silver to finance their activities. The Athenian fleet landed the army to the north of Syracuse and took control of the heights of Epipolai, a plateau above the city. From there they set about building siege walls. The Syracusans tried building counter-walls to prevent their city being entirely cut off from the land. In a battle to wrest control of the Syracusan fortifications Lamachos was separated from the main Athenian forces with only a few other hoplites around him. A Syracusan officer called Kallikrates then challenged him to single combat; they both killed each other, but the Syracusans easily overcame Lamachos' companions and took his body, stripping the armour from it and taking it back to the city. Nikias, who was too ill to participate in the main battle, managed to beat off an attack on the main Athenian fortifications and the Syracusans were then

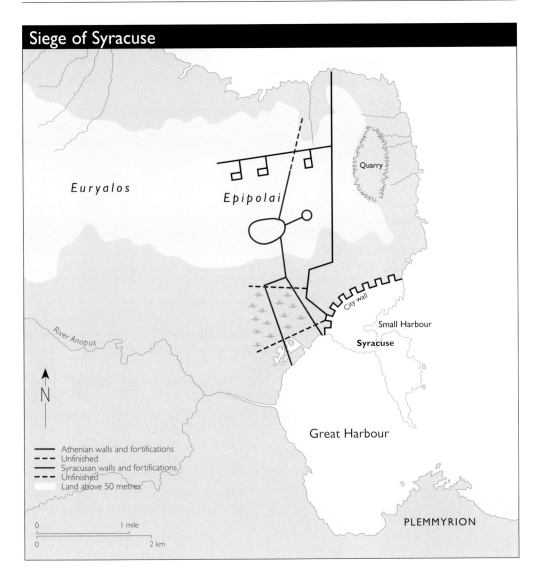

Siege of Syracuse

Euryalos

Epipolai

Quarry

River Anapus

City wall

Small Harbour

Syracuse

N

Great Harbour

PLEMMYRION

—— Athenian walls and fortifications
- - - Unfinished
—— Syracusan walls and fortifications
- - - Unfinished
 Land above 50 metres

0   I mile
0   2 km

dismayed to see the Athenian fleet sailing into their Great Harbour.

The Syracusans had sent urgent messages to the Peloponnese asking for assistance and Corinth, as the mother-city of Syracuse, had pressed the Spartans to act. Corinth and Sparta sent only a few ships and troops, but the Spartans supplied a determined and resourceful commander in the mould of Brasidas. His name was Gylippos. It was the news of his arrival, slipping past the ships that Nikias belatedly sent to try to intercept him, that halted discussions among the disheartened Syracusans about negotiating a truce with Nikias. Gylippos managed to

gather some soldiers from other parts of Sicily and he encouraged the Syracusans to take the offensive, inflicting the first significant defeat on the Athenians through his skilful use of cavalry. The Syracusans continued with their counter-walls and succeeded in building them out to a point where the Athenians were unable to complete their circumvallation of the city. While the Syracusans began training their naval forces to take on the Athenians, Gylippos went in search of more reinforcements. Nikias also decided that help was needed and he sent a letter back to the Athenians asking either for permission to return home or for massive reinforcements.

He also requested a replacement general because a serious kidney disease was making it difficult for him to carry out his duties.

Athenian defeat in Sicily

In view of their ambition and determination in the earlier stages of the war, it is no great surprise that the Athenians rejected the idea of recalling the whole expedition. Nor did they allow Nikias to step down, but they did appoint two of his officers to assist him and, more importantly, they sent Demosthenes, the hero of Sphakteria, to Syracuse with a large fleet of reinforcements. Before these forces arrived, however, Gylippos and the Syracusans managed to seize the main forts and stores at Plemmyrion on the southern side of the Great Harbour after a combined land and sea operation. This defeat forced the Athenians to crowd into an inadequate camp in unhealthy, marshy ground on the west side of the Great Harbour.

The Syracusans also modified their triremes to utilise a new tactic against the highly

A silver coin from Syracuse dating to about 400 and showing, beneath the main image of a chariot racing victory, a trophy of captured armour. Such trophies were usually erected at the site of a battle by the winning side, using armour from the defeated enemy. This coin may be meant to commemorate the defeat of the Athenians in 413. (Ancient Art and Architecture)

skilled Athenians. The Syracusans adopted a Corinthian idea that involved shortening the bow sections of their triremes and fitting extra beams across the hulls at the point where the anchors were usually housed. The effect of this was to transform the sleek, sharp-prowed vessels designed for penetrating the vulnerable hulls of enemy triremes, into stockier, blunt-nosed ships which were capable of ramming the lighter-built Athenian ships head on and disabling them, without being badly damaged themselves. In the relatively confined waters of the Great Harbour at Syracuse such tactics were far more effective than those employed by the Athenians, who preferred to row round an enemy ship and strike them from the side or rear.

When the Syracusans were ready to try out their new tactics they also used another Corinthian stratagem. They challenged the Athenians at sea in the morning and then broke off, apparently giving up for the day; but they had arranged for food to be brought directly to shore so that their crews could take a quick meal and then set out again while the Athenians were unprepared and hungry. In the fighting which followed many of the Athenian triremes were badly damaged by the heavy prows of the Syracusan ships and seven were lost completely.

Just when things were looking bleak for Nikias and his men, however, Demosthenes sailed into the Great Harbour with 73 ships, 5,000 hoplites and thousands of light infantry. With his characteristic decisiveness Demosthenes recommended a strong attack on the Syracusan counter-walls, but this was beaten off. A risky night attack from the heights of Euryalos attempted to take the fortifications in the rear, but the Syracusans, reinforced with non-Spartan troops from Lakonia and 300 elite Boiotian hoplites, routed the Athenians and drove them back once more. Demosthenes concluded that there was now no alternative but to abandon the siege and sail back to Athens. Nikias took some persuading, however, since he was still hopeful of getting a negotiated surrender through the activities of pro-Athenian faction within Syracuse, and he expected that the

Assembly would blame him for the expedition's failure. However, the situation was made worse for the Athenians by the arrival of more allies to help the Syracusans and Nikias agreed to depart. Just as the Athenians were about to leave, however, an eclipse of the moon occurred. Nikias and many of the Athenians took this as an omen that the gods disapproved of their plans and some diviners among them prescribed a wait of 27 days before deciding what to do next.

The Syracusans took the initiative once more. First they challenged the Athenians to another battle and destroyed 18 of their ships, wiping out the numerical advantage that Demosthenes' arrival had created. Then they blockaded the entrance to the Great Harbour, which was less than a mile wide. The Athenians tried to force their way through, but they were so comprehensively defeated that the following day the Syracusans were able to tow away the surviving Athenian ships without any resistance. The Athenians were demoralised, exhausted and dangerously short of supplies. There was no alternative now but to attempt a retreat overland to a friendly Sicilian community in the interior of the island. They abandoned their sick and wounded and set off in two columns, one led by Demosthenes and the other by Nikias. The Syracusans caught them up, however, and Demosthenes quickly surrendered, after being given assurances that the men would not be starved or executed. Nikias' men tried to push on, but when they finally reached a watercourse their discipline broke and they became easy prey for the Syracusans and their allies, who set about slaughtering them in the river bed. Nikias, who had worked so hard to make peace between Athens and Sparta, surrendered to Gylippos, in the hope that the Spartan's influence would prevent him from being executed. It did not, as the Corinthians were eager to prevent him being ransomed and some of the Syracusans wanted to ensure that he did not reveal, under torture, details of their earlier negotiations to hand over the city to the Athenians. He and Demosthenes were

executed and the rest of the survivors were shut up in the nearby quarries for 70 days, where many of them died of exposure and starvation. Eventually most of them were sold as slaves. Page 78 recounts how some of them managed to get back home.

News of the defeat was slow in reaching Athens and when it did the Athenians could scarcely believe that their magnificent invasion force had been totally destroyed. The first person to bring news of the disaster seems to have been a travelling merchant who disembarked in the Peiraieus and went to a barber's shop. There he began chatting to the barber about it, assuming that it was common knowledge. The barber, on realising what he was referring to, ran up to the city and rushed into the market place to tell the magistrates what he had heard. They convened a meeting of the people's assembly and presented the barber before them with his story. Because the man could not give a satisfactory explanation of the source of his information – he did not know the stranger's name or where he had heard the news – he was assumed to be an agitator deliberately spreading malicious rumours. Indeed, he was being tortured to reveal more of his supposed plot when further messengers arrived with full details of the events.

Dekeleia

After his arrival in Sparta Alkibiades had recommended that the Peloponnesians take a leaf from the Athenians' book of strategies by seizing and occupying a fortress in Athenian territory. He suggested Dekeleia on the southern slopes of Mt Parnes, but the Spartans were reluctant to commit themselves to offensive action while the Peace of Nikias was potentially still valid. In the summer of 414, however, an Athenian fleet of 30 ships was assisting the Argives in their ongoing border war with Sparta and it made several incursions into Lakonian territory. The Spartans were satisfied that the enemy had violated the treaty and prepared to march out and occupy Dekeleia the following spring.

When Agis and the Peloponnesians invaded Attika in 413 they opened a new phase in the war. Instead of ravaging as much as they could of the Athenians' territory for a short while and then going home, they now set up a permanent garrison in the fort of Dekeleia. From there they made raids across large parts of Attika. The Athenians had to disperse their military strength in garrisons of their own, but much of their agricultural land was rendered too vulnerable to farm, and they were prevented from using the overland route from Oropos to bring in supplies from the island of Euboia. This had been a key source of food for the city of Athens during the Archidamian War, and was one reason for the Athenians' ability to continue the struggle far longer than their enemies had expected. They could still bring resources into Athens, but now they had to come by sea, round Cape Sounion and into the harbour at Peiraieus. A further effect of the occupation of Dekeleia was to encourage slaves to escape from their masters and take refuge in Dekeleia. Thucydides estimated that 20,000 such runaways fled from the towns, farms and, above all, the silver mines of Southern Attika.

Even this increase in pressure on the Athenian homeland was not enough to force them to come to terms with the Spartans. As long as they could draw on the extensive resources of their maritime empire they could continue the war. In order to deprive them of access to these resources the Spartans and their allies had to mount a major naval offensive in the Eastern Aegean. They began this task in 412/411, when several of Athens' key allies defected, after the news of the Sicilian disaster reached them and they realised that Athens had been severely weakened. In 412 the Spartans received a welcome boost to their own naval strength with the arrival of 25 Syracusan ships, but the bulk of their fleets had to be provided by Sparta and her Peloponnesian allies, especially Corinth. The cost of this sustained naval effort was beyond them, so Sparta had to persuade the king of Persia to fund and support her overseas operations. Even with Persian aid it still took another seven years before Athenian resistance was worn down and their last fleet was captured in the Hellespont.

These ancient stone quarries near Syracuse were used to imprison and punish the Athenians captured after the defeat of the Sicilian expedition in 413, many of whom died there from exposure and starvation. Most of those who survived were sold as slaves. (AKG Berlin)

A ship's captain at war

The trials of a young trierarch

Some of the best sources of information on individual Athenians are the written versions of speeches delivered in the law courts. Several of these give details of the military activities of specific people during the Peloponnesian War. One of the most detailed of these accounts derives from a speech made by a defendant who was put on trial in the year 403/402 for embezzlement of public funds. If found guilty he would be stripped of his citizen rights and his property. As part of his defence he recited his war record to the court.

Athenian trials normally took place at one of several designated sites in or near the Agora, the main market place in Athens, which was surrounded by public buildings. They were presided over by an official called an *archon* whose main function was to ensure that proper procedures were followed. Verdicts were decided by the votes of a jury consisting of Athenian citizens, aged over 30, who had registered themselves for a year and volunteered to act as jurors on the day. Two hundred or more jurors would be assigned to each court in the morning and they might hear several cases in a day. From the middle of the fifth century they were paid two obols for the day, a measure proposed by Perikles. This was later raised to three obols, on the proposal of Kleon, but it was still far less than a strong, healthy man might be able to earn for a day's work. Consequently many of the volunteers were men who were short of money or unfit for hard work, particularly the poor and elderly. *The Wasps*, a famous comic play written by Aristophanes characterises the jurors as bad-tempered old men who attended the courts for the money and the chance to inflict punishments on the rich and powerful. For cases involving

major political issues a meeting of the citizen assembly sometimes acted as a law court.

An Athenian trial was essentially a contest between the prosecutor and the defendant, each of whom attempted to persuade the jury to vote in their favour. They were given a certain period of time to put their case and they had to speak for themselves. The speakers would, as in a modern trial, try to prove guilt or innocence of the specific charge by referring to known facts, citing evidence and offering the statements of witnesses. They might also argue that the interpretation of a particular law did or did not allow it to be applied in this case, but they were also able to make more generalised arguments about themselves or their opponents which most modern courts would not allow. The large number of jurors and the random allotment to courts made it impossible to bribe the jury, but the prosecutors and defendants might try to gain their sympathy, flatter them, or appeal to their sense of self-interest in order to secure a favourable verdict. At the time of the Peloponnesian War it was becoming common for litigants to hire someone to write a persuasive speech for them. For this case the defendant hired Lysias, the son of Kephalos, a non-Athenian businessman who had considerable skills as a speech writer. The speech he composed for this defendant was preserved and later published along with many others written by Lysias. Most of what follows is directly attested in the speech; other details are deduced from the speech and a combination of other historical sources, mainly Xenophon's *Hellenika*.

The name of the defendant in this particular trial is not known, but we do learn that he was a sponsor of dramatic choruses (*choregos*) and a trierarch. This means that he was one of the wealthiest Athenian citizens.

This fragment of a Classical Athenian marble relief clearly shows the three levels of oars which propelled a trireme. Only the topmost level of oarsmen are visible, because they rowed through an outrigger, whereas the lower two put their oars through ports in the side of the ship's hull. Constant practice was needed to co-ordinate the efforts of up to 170 oarsmen on each ship and the Athenians prided themselves on having the best trained crews in Greece. (Debra de Souza)

The duty of a *choregos* was to supervise and pay for the training and performance of a festival chorus, a group of singers and dancers who would take part in one of the many public religious festivals of the Athenians. By spending lavishly on these choruses, and hopefully winning prizes, a wealthy man could gain much prestige and goodwill from his fellow citizens.

The main duties of a trierarch were to ensure that the trireme assigned to him was fully equipped, properly crewed and operationally effective throughout the campaign period. These were primarily financial obligations. The basic wages for the crew, plus a daily maintenance allowance so that each man could buy provisions, were supposed to be paid from the state funds allocated for each particular expedition or campaign. But the money available to the generals in command of the fleet was often inadequate, forcing the trierarchs to meet the immediate costs out of their own resources.

In order to prevent the crews from spending too much money on things which might make them unfit for service, such as wine and unhealthy foods, the Athenians usually allowed only half of the wages to be paid whilst the ships were active, with the rest being handed over when they returned to Peiraieus at the end of the campaign. When manpower was in short supply, however, the trierarchs could be tempted to offer full pay, or additional bonuses in order to attract skilled sailors or experienced oarsmen. The young trierarch emphasised at his trial the extra amounts of money he spent on his ship and his crew to ensure that they were the best in the fleet.

A trierarch was normally expected to command the ship in person, although there was no guarantee that he would have appropriate military experience or navigational competence. Lysias' client claims to have inflicted great damage on enemy ships during the various sea battles in which he was involved, but that claim is not supported with any details and is exactly the sort of thing he might expected to say in order to make the jurors think well of him. In practice an inexperienced trierarch will have relied upon the knowledge and judgment of his helmsman or *kubernetes*, who was usually a professional sailor. A very experienced, skilful helmsman could demand that a trierarch pay very high wages for his services. Ideally the trierarch and his helmsman would form a close partnership, which is exactly what Lysias' client had to do when hiring a renowned helmsman called Phantias, who stayed with his ship for seven years.

The defendant was very young, having only recently come of age and passed the formal scrutiny, or *dokimasia* which all young men had to undergo before they could be officially entered on the rolls of Athenian citizens. It normally took place in their eighteenth or nineteenth year and involved checking the candidate's entitlement to participate in the public life of the city. The defendant's first term as a trierarch seems to have been in the Athenian

year 411/410. He continued in this capacity for the next seven years, participating in a series of naval battles in which the Athenians experienced both resounding success and abject failure. By reciting his record of service as a trierarch in the recent war the defendant hoped to win the sympathy of the jury. He could argue that for the jury to convict him, depriving him of his property and his citizen rights would only harm their own interests. He could do far more for them if he remained a wealthy citizen, than if he lost his citizenship and all his property.

The generals' favourite

The young trierarch's war service started when the charismatic Athenian general Alkibiades was resuming his military career. He was elected as one of the 10 generals for the Athenian year 411/410 and took a position of joint command over the fleet which was operating in the Aegean. Alkibiades was notorious for his luxurious lifestyle, even when on campaign. He was wealthy enough to maintain his own trireme, with his close friend Antiochos as its helmsman. Rather than place his bedroll on the ship's deck, as the other officers and trierarchs did, he had a section of the deck cut away to make a large cabin area wherein he hung a hammock to provide him with a more comfortable night's sleep. Once he had joined the main Athenian fleet, however, Alkibiades decided to make use of the young trierarch's well maintained vessel. He liked to lead detachments of the fastest ships from the fleet to lure the enemy into an ambush, or to make swift surprise attacks against enemy bases and coastal cities. He could have done this in his own trireme, but he seems to have preferred to use the trierarch's vessel on these occasions, presumably because it was faster and had a better crew. The next few years of the war saw an upturn in the fortunes of the Athenians under Alkibiades, with several minor victories and a major triumph over the Peloponnesian fleet at Kyzikos in 410.

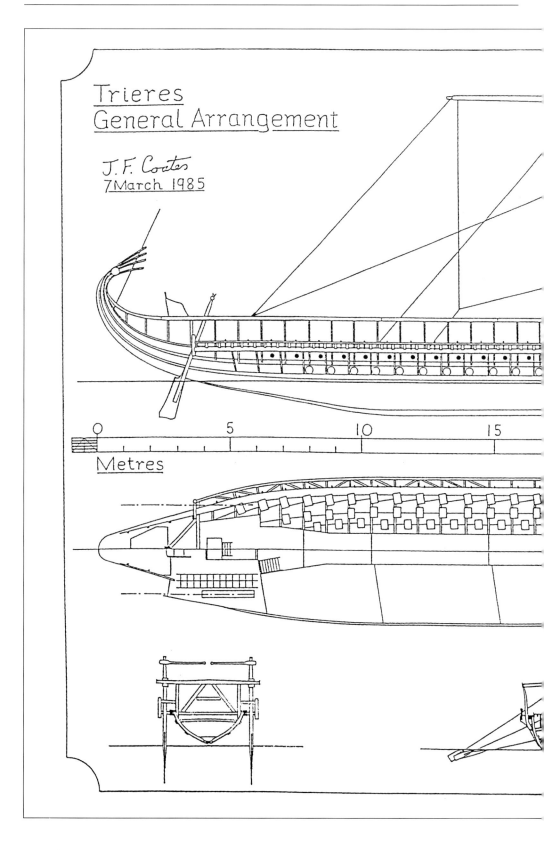

Trieres
General Arrangement

J. F. Coates
7 March 1985

0   5   10   15

Metres

This drawing by the naval architect J F Coates shows the
general arrangement of his reconstruction of a typical
Athenian trireme. The hull is long, narrow and sits quite
high in the water; the ram protrudes forward of the bow
at the waterline. The oarsmens' seats are very close
together and there is little space for carrying soldiers and
supplies. (J F Coates)

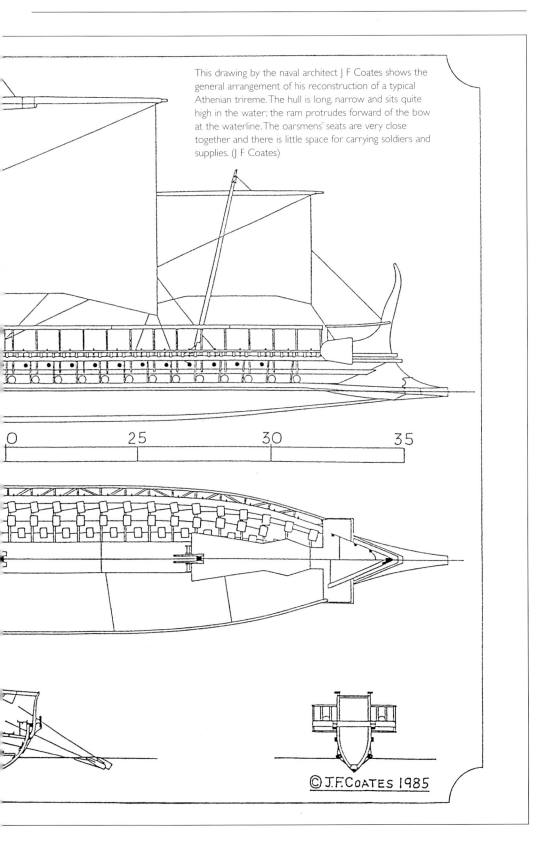

© J.F.COATES 1985

This Athenian gravestone bears the name Demokleides, son of Demetrios and depicts
a lone man seated above the prow of a trireme. Many Athenian and allied citizens were
lost at sea in the Peloponnesian War. Their relatives were often upset at not being able
to conduct proper funerals rituals for them. (Ancient Art and Architecture)

The young trierarch told the jury at his trial, 'I would have done anything not to have him sailing with me.' He pointed out that he was not related to Alkibiades, nor were they friends, or even members of the same tribe, but he was forced to accept him on board the ship because he was the overall commander of the fleet. It may well be, however, that the trierarch was exaggerating his dislike for Alkibiades in order to avoid seeming to have been too closely associated with someone who had fallen out of favour on two occasions. The jury at the trierarch's trial would have contained some passionate supporters of the restored democracy, who might consider Alkibiades a traitor and take a similar attitude to anyone who was closely associated with him.

Early in 406 the trierarch's ship was once more detached from the main fleet, now based at Notion, while Alkibiades sailed to join in an attack on the city of Phokaia. Against Alkibiades' instructions, his personal helmsman, Antiochos, who had been left in charge of the main fleet, got into a battle with the Spartan fleet under Lysandros and was defeated with the loss of 22 ships. This defeat was only a setback for the Athenians, but it provided an opportunity for Alkibiades' rivals and enemies to bring his dominance to an end. Back in Athens he was blamed for the defeat and heavily criticised for entrusting command of the main fleet to Antiochos, a mere helmsman. A new board of 10 generals was elected and Alkibiades was not one of them. Several citizens threatened to take out lawsuits against him, which they could easily do once he ceased to be a general. Understanding that his popularity and influence had been so badly undermined that any jury in Athens was likely to be very hostile, he took his own trireme and sailed off to his private fortresses in the Hellespont.

The young trierarch now had a new general on board, Archestratos, one of those who had been elected following the downfall of Alkibiades. In the summer of 406 Archestratos ordered the trierarch to sail with Konon's (the new commander) fleet from Samos to try to prevent the new Spartan commander, Kallikratidas, from capturing the city of Methymna on the island of Lesbos. Archestratos, the general who was sailing on the trierarch's ship, was killed at this point and yet another of the Athenian generals, Erasinides, commandeered the trierarch's vessel for his own use. Soon afterwards the Spartan fleet was defeated by the Athenians in a major sea battle off the Arginousai islands, but Erasinides and five of his fellow generals were tried and executed back in Athens for failing to rescue the crews of the stricken Athenian ships.

The young trierarch's next major battle was the disastrous defeat at Aigospotamoi, in the summer of 405. On this occasion the Athenian fleet was attacked by the Spartans while the crews were dispersed looking for supplies. The young trierarch was in full command of his ship on this occasion, having no general on board, and his crew were not caught napping, probably because he spent extra money to ensure that there were plenty of supplies available to them without the need for extended foraging. His experienced helmsman, Phantias, may also have advised him to keep his crew in a state of readiness. As a result of his preparedness, when the Spartans attacked he was able to get his trireme away and to rescue another Athenian ship as well. All but a handful of ships from the Athenian fleet were captured by the Spartans and the Athenian citizens among their crews were executed. Soon afterwards the Athenians, with their city now blockaded by land and sea surrendered to the Spartans.

Buying the goodwill of the people

The defendant proudly claimed to have spent the huge sum of six talents during his time as a trierarch, which was far more than was legally required. Patriotic fervour may partly account for this, but there are hints in his speech that he had other motives for being so generous on behalf of his fellow-

Battle of Arginousai, phase one

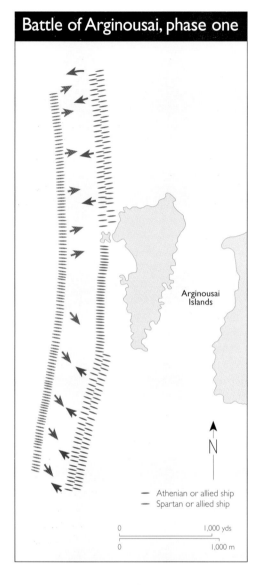

Arginousai
Islands

N

— Athenian or allied ship
— Spartan or allied ship

0   1,000 yds
0   1,000 m

LEFT AND RIGHT

1. The Athenians drew up their 155 ships with two groups of 60, one on each wing and 35 in the centre. The ships on the wings were arranged in two staggered lines, one behind the other, to discourage the Spartans from breaking through the line to attack ships from the side or rear. Those in the centre used the westernmost of the Arginousai islands to protect them. The Athenian wings moved forward while their centre held station. The 120 ships in the Spartan fleet feared that they might be outflanked and attacked from the side or rear, because the Athenian lines extended beyond theirs. So they moved away from the centre and engaged the wings, gradually separating into two sections.

2. After a fierce battle the Spartan left wing was defeated, Kallikratidas was killed and the surviving ships fled south. The Spartan right wing fought harder, but it was also defeated. As the Spartans fled the 35 ships in the Athenian centre joined in the pursuit. The Spartans lost 77 ships while the Athenians lost only 25.

brief struggle between oligarchic and democratic factions among the Athenian fleet at Samos. This would explain why Lysias' speech fails to mention any patriotic deeds performed by the father on behalf of the Athenians. It was better to avoid all mention of a man whose record was suspect and concentrate instead on the zealous contributions of his son to the Athenian cause.

The young trierarch's own political sympathies are only hinted at, but they seem also to have been oligarchic, rather than particularly democratic. At his trial he tried to distance himself from Alkibiades, who was one of the instigators of the oligarchic revolution in 411, but he could not hide the fact that the infamous general spent a lot of time on his ship. They were both very wealthy men, with a marked preference for the best that money could buy and may have become good friends. The trierarch was very vague about his own activities in the crucial year 404/403, when Athens was under the control of the so-called Thirty Tyrants, a ruthless and unpopular oligarchic government imposed by the Spartans after the Athenians surrendered. He continued to perform his public liturgies and at the very least it seems that the oligarchs made no attempt to condemn him and confiscate his property, which they did to many of their political opponents.

citizens. It is very likely that the young trierarch's father was actively involved in the oligarchic revolution of 411. Like his son he would have been a very wealthy man and probably also served as trierarch. Thucydides says that the trierarchs with the fleet at Samos played a major part in plotting the overthrow of the democracy back at Athens and the young trierarch's father may even have been a member of the infamous council of 400, a group of wealthy citizens who took control of affairs in Athens for several months in 411. The circumstances of his death are not mentioned, but it may have occurred in the

Battle of Arginousai, phase two

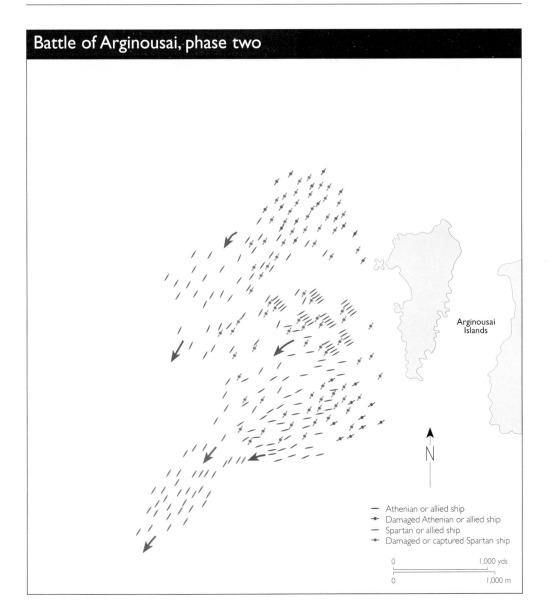

Arginousai
Islands

N

— Athenian or allied ship
→ Damaged Athenian or allied ship
— Spartan or allied ship
→ Damaged or captured Spartan ship

0   1,000 yds

0   1,000 m

How typical were the wartime experiences of this particular trierarch? In terms of his participation in raids and battles there was nothing unusual, although other trierarchs would not have had to play host to a succession of generals on their ships. To have served as a trierarch for seven consecutive years was highly unusual, however, and it cannot be a coincidence that in this particular case the seven years were, in effect, the last years of the war. The financial position of the Athenians had deteriorated as the war dragged on. From 413 they were

losing the revenues of their maritime empire as more and more states defected to the Spartans, whether willingly or under duress. The cost of combating this was enormous, as it involved maintaining fleets and armies overseas all year round. The trierarch also paid large contributions to the war tax during this period and he was one of many wealthy citizens who must have felt that they were being made to bear the financial costs of the belligerent policies of the less wealthy majority of citizens. This was one reason why so many of the trierarchs supported the oligarchic revolution in 411 which promised to make peace with the Spartans.

We do not know the outcome of the trial. The defendant had been accused of embezzlement, but there is no reason to think he was guilty. He hints in his speech that his opponent has been put on trial recently on charges of impiety. Accusations made for personal or political rivalry were common in Athens and prominent men could expect to face several during their lives.

Politics and culture

Democracy and oligarchy

The Peloponnesian War affected the lives of most of the people in the Greek world at the end of the fifth century BC. One of the most important political effects of the long war between Athens and Sparta was the polarisation of much of the Greek world into blocks of allies and supporters of either the Athenians or the Spartans. Many of the states involved in the war adopted or retained political constitutions that were similar to that of the state to which they were allied. Those on the Spartan side tended to have oligarchic constitutions, whereas the allies of Athens tended to favour democracy. The Spartans found it much easier to deal with oligarchies than democracies. They were suspicious of large citizen bodies with broad decision making powers, whereas the Athenians saw such groups of people as their natural allies, and vice versa. The Spartans claimed to be fighting the Athenians in order to 'liberate' the Greeks from their tyrannical rule, but the form that they preferred this liberation to take was often the repression of a broadly based, democratic regime and its replacement by a much narrower oligarchic one. As the war dragged on many cities were subject to revolutionary changes, according to whether a pro-Spartan or a pro-Athenian faction had the upper hand. The result was a series of parallel conflicts that raged in many of the city-states of Greece. Thucydides wrote a scathing condemnation of these civil wars in his account of the Peloponnesian War. He blamed them on people whose ambitions and lust for power, coupled with fanatical devotion to their political friends, made them blind to the need for moderation and compromise in their dealings with their fellow-citizens. The widespread tendency to exact revenge for each atrocity simply prolonged the hatred.

We noted on pp. 28-30 how the dispute over Epidamnos escalated to such an extent that Corcyra became involved in a war with Corinth. Corcyra in turn drew the Athenians into this war, and eventually through Corinth the Spartans became embroiled as well. Athenian expeditions intervened in the internal affairs of Corcyra in 427 and 425 on behalf of the democratic faction, who drove their oligarchic opponents out of the city. The exiled oligarchic faction established themselves on the mainland opposite Corcyra and launched piratical raids on the territory held by their opponents. They tried to persuade the Corinthians and the Spartans to take up their cause once again and restore them to power by force, but without success. Eventually they decided to abandon their mainland bases and cross back over to the island. They established a fortified base in the mountains to the north of the city and continued their guerrilla attacks from there, with the aim of preventing the democratic faction from gaining control of the countryside and encouraging the rest of the citizens to demand a change of government. The Athenians continued to maintain contact with their allies in Corcyra and used the island as a staging point for their expeditions to Sicily.

In 410 the leaders of the pro-Athenian, democratic faction in Corcyra feared that their opponents were about to establish a new oligarchic constitution, with military backing from the Spartans. To forestall this they invited the Athenian general Konon to come from his base at Naupaktos and take control of the city. Konon brought with him a force of 600 Messenian exiles, hereditary enemies of the Spartans, who carried out a ruthless slaughter of many of the leading oligarchs in Corcyra and drove over 1,000 others out of the city. They were forced to take refuge on the mainland, opposite Corcyra. Konon and his force then withdrew, leaving the democratic faction in power. In an effort to preserve their numerical superiority they made many slaves and foreigners citizens of the *polis*, hoping that they would be staunch supporters of the democratic constitution. The remaining members of the oligarchic faction would not give in, however, and after the Athenians and Messenians had gone they occupied the market place in the centre of the city and encouraged their exiled comrades to return. After a day of bitter fighting in the city the survivors of both groups decided that their murderous quarrel had gone on long enough and agreed to put aside their differences and try to live together in harmony. The remaining citizens of Corcyra, realising how much death and destruction had been caused by allowing outsiders to become involved in their affairs, decided to keep out of the war and not to ally themselves with either Athens or Sparta.

Persia

The most significant royal power to become involved in the Peloponnesian War was the king of Persia. The king of Persia was known to the Greeks as the Great King. He ruled an enormous empire that stretched from Asia Minor and Egypt in the west to India and Afghanistan in the east. Most provinces of this empire paid an annual tribute of silver to the king's treasury in Persepolis. This tribute had been paid by many of the Greeks of western Asia Minor and the Aegean until 478, when they began making payments to the Delian League instead. But the wealth of the Persian Empire far exceeded that of all of the Greek states put together.

It is likely that both the Athenians and the Persians tried to persuade the Persian king to intervene on their side from the very start of the war. The Athenians had been making war on the territory of the Persian Empire since 478, but they made a peace treaty with the Persian king in 449 and were probably prepared to negotiate concessions

of territory or tribute in return for his aid against the Spartans. In 424 an Athenian naval patrol captured a Persian envoy called Artaphernes who was on his way to Sparta. The Persian king, Artaxerxes, was fed up with receiving contradictory requests and messages from successive Spartan envoys and he wanted Artaphernes to return with a definitive proposal. The Athenians tried to use the opportunity to put their own proposals to the Great King, but Artaxerxes died before their envoys reached his court. There was a brief but violent struggle over the succession, but eventually a new, strong king, Dareios II emerged and the Athenians were able to renew their peaceful relations with him.

In 414/413 Pissouthnes, one of the Persian king's governors or *satraps* in Asia Minor revolted. He obtained some Athenian assistance, but the Athenian general Lykon betrayed him to the Persian king. His illegitimate son, Amorges, continued the revolt and the Athenians helped him as well. As a result the Great King ordered another of his satraps, Tissaphernes, to make arrangements to aid the Spartans. In spite of their repeated claim to be fighting in order to liberate the Greeks, the Spartans negotiated a series of treaties with the representatives of King Dareios in which they agreed that those territories in Asia Minor which had formerly been under Persian domination should revert to his control. This included many Greek cities that had joined the Delian League under Athenian leadership in 478 and were now looking to Sparta to free them from Athenian domination. In return the king's men promised to help the Spartans with money, ships and men. This assistance was to prove decisive in bringing the war to an end.

Arts and culture in Athens

The period from the end of the Persian Wars to the end of the Peloponnesian War has often been called the Golden Age of Athens.

A gold coin of the Persian Empire from the fourth century. The design shows a Persian king carrying a bow and a spear, both traditional Persian weapons for war and hunting. Many Persian gold coins came to Greece as 'gifts' for those Greeks who were prepared to do the Great King's bidding. (AKG Berlin)

The city became one of the major cultural and artistic centres of the Classical Greek world. The most obvious manifestation of this was the magnificent temples and other public buildings which adorned the city. There is some evidence that the Athenians were criticised for spending money which, it was claimed, they had obtained from their subject allies to beautify their own city, which the critics compared to a woman decking herself out in expensive jewels. In response to such critics Perikles is said to have argued that it was not necessary to give an account of how all the money was spent. It was only fair, he claimed, if Athens used any surpluses that remained after the expenses of war were met to build works that would bring her glory for all time. He was certainly right in his prediction that such buildings would serve to perpetuate the fame of Athens well into the future. As Thucydides pointed out, in contrast to Athens Sparta had no magnificent public buildings and anyone comparing the remains of the two cities in future ages would find it hard to believe that they had been equally powerful.

This model reconstructs a temple on the Athenian Acropolis which was built between 447 and 438. It was dedicated to Athena the Maiden, or Athena *Parthenos* in Greek, hence it is called the Parthenon. It was designed by Pheidias and contained a statue covered in ivory and gold. In an emergency the god could be removed, melted down and turned into coins. (Ancient Art and Architecture)

It is not just for her buildings that fifth-century Athens has achieved lasting fame. The exquisite painted cups and vases produced by her master potters were exported across the Mediterranean, particularly to Italy and Sicily and are still considered to be among the great works of

art of the Western world. Athens was also a
major centre for literature, rhetoric and
philosophy. Many writers and philosophers
from other Greek cities visited Athens, but
probably the most famous literary figures of
the Periklean age are the Athenian born
writers of tragic and comic plays.

Euripides

Among the works of the great Athenian
playwrights those of Euripides stand out as
the most effective at conveying to modern
audiences the emotions and passions of the
time. This may be partly because his plays
often focus on women as either the victims
or avengers of violent acts. Many of his plays
were written during the Peloponnesian War.
In one of them, *The Trojan Women*,
performed at the Great Festival of Dionysos
in 415, Euripides offered his Athenian
audience a chilling perspective on
contemporary events. In the previous
summer the Athenians had invaded the
island of Melos in the Southern Aegean. The
Melians were distantly related to the Spartans
and had tried to maintain a position of
neutrality, but the Athenians laid siege to
their city and starved them into surrender.
The citizen men were massacred and the
women and children were sold into slavery.
As was traditional for Athenian tragedies,
Euripides based his play on an old, familiar
story, the 10-year siege of Troy by the Greeks
under their great king, Agamemnon. On this
occasion, however, he chose to set the play in
the immediate aftermath of the fall of Troy,
when the Greeks had achieved their objective
and recovered Helen, the stolen wife of
Agamemnon's brother Menelaus, and were
deciding what to do with the captured
women of Troy and their children. This
setting provided an opportunity for Euripides
to present his audience with a view of how
these women might feel as they
contemplated a future as slaves of their
conquerors.

We cannot be sure how the Athenians
reacted to a play that invited them to
sympathise with the helpless victims of war.
Many of the men in the audience will have
bought women or children from Melos as
slaves. It has been suggested that the play
failed to win first prize because it was so
relevant to the current situation and its
emotional impact was too painful for the
Athenians to bear.

We know that Euripides' plays were famous across the whole of the Greek speaking world. Each new text was circulated among the Greek-speaking cities of the Mediterranean and many people learnt sections or even whole plays by heart. His verses were particularly popular among the Greeks of Sicily, whose delight in them was so great that Athenian prisoners captured and enslaved by the Syracusans in 413 were able to obtain better treatment by reciting extracts from the plays to their captors. Some were even said to have gained their freedom in return for teaching their masters all they could recall of Euripides' works. When they eventually returned home to Athens they visited Euripides to thank him in person. Euripides himself never seems to have been entirely at ease living in Athens. He was invited to Macedon towards the end of the Peloponnesian War and he remained there until he died in 407.

Euripides offers a woman's view
In this extract from Euripides' play, The Trojan Women, *Andromache, widow of the Trojan prince Hektor, who was slain by the Greek hero Achilles, learns that she is to be taken by Achilles' son, who wants her as his wife:*

'I will be enslaved in the household of my own people's killer, and if I put Hektor's love out of my mind and open my heart to this new husband I shall be seen to dishonour the dead. But the alternative is to hate and be hated by my own master. And yet they say that a single, sweet night removes the woman's dislike for her man's bed. I disown any woman who rejects her former husband to devote herself to a new love. Even a mare who has been uncoupled from her stable-companion does not readily take up the yoke. And yet dumb animals lack rational minds and are inferior to us by nature.' (ll. 659-671)

Hipparete, an Athenian citizen woman

Childhood in Athens

Although we have only limited evidence for the lives of non-combatants in the Peloponnesian War, it is possible to put together information from a variety of sources to present an account of how an individual's life might have been affected by the war. One such individual is Hipparete, the wife of the Athenian politician and general Alkibiades. Hipparete was born about 440. She was the daughter of a prominent Athenian citizen, Hipponikos, whose family owned a large amount of land in Attika and obtained considerable revenue from the silver mining industry. Indeed, he was reputed to be the richest man in Greece. Hipparete's mother, whose name is not known, had previously been married to the famous Perikles, but they were divorced in about 455 and she married Hipponikos soon after.

Hipparete's childhood was as comfortable and happy as was possible for the daughter of a citizen. Upper class Athenian girls led quiet, sheltered lives, surrounded by women and only occasionally venturing out of their homes to participate in religious festivals, particularly those associated with Athena, the patron goddess of the Athenians. In the words of one Athenian writer, Xenophon, the daughter of a wealthy citizen was expected to be raised, 'under careful supervision, so that she might see and hear and speak as little as possible.' Hipparete spent most of her childhood under the watchful eyes of her slave nurse and her mother, learning the skills considered appropriate for a young woman. These included cooking, spinning, weaving and caring for the sick. Since her family was wealthy she may even have learned to read and write, although such education was not considered necessary or even desirable for girls, whose upbringing was geared towards preparing them to be capable but subservient wives.

War and plague

The outbreak of the Peloponnesian War must have had a profound effect on Hipparete's life. The city in which she was growing up would have changed, both in appearance and in atmosphere. It was already becoming more densely populated, both in the main urban centre around the Acropolis, and the secondary area of Peiraieus. The increased prosperity which had accompanied Athens' expanding imperial power and flourishing maritime trade encouraged people from near and far to come and live there.

Perikles' strategy of avoiding pitched battles with the invading Peloponnesian armies resulted in many families having to abandon the countryside around Athens and move within the fortifications of the Long Walls. The narrow strips of land between the walls became home to many thousands of refugees, who built houses and cultivated the ground to try to compensate for the loss of their agricultural resources, which were at the mercy of the invaders. Their numbers were swelled by refugees from Plataia, who arrived in the city in the summer of 431, after an attack by the Thebans had demonstrated their city's vulnerability.

The crowded, unsanitary conditions, especially in the hot, dry summers, must have made the city a particularly unpleasant place for these refugees to live. In 430, when a deadly plague broke out in Athens, life there became much worse. The plague reached Athens from the East, having already

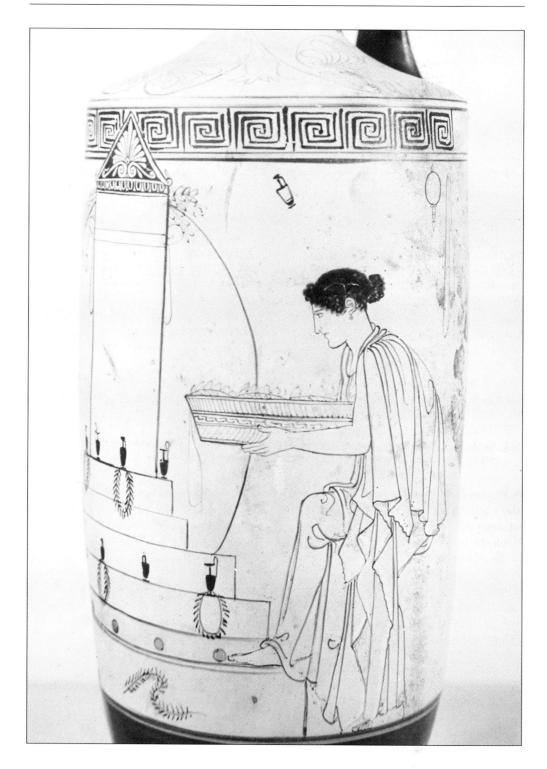

An Athenian painted vase from the mid-fifth century, showing a woman placing
wreaths on a grave. This kind of small vase was commonly used for pouring libations
at a graveside. The painting shows several similar vases on the steps of the grave
monument, which probably marks a family burial plot. (Ancient Art and Architecture)

ravaged parts of the Persian Empire. The very maritime traders whose business was so vital to the city's economy also provided transport for the lethal bacteria. Initially the plague struck in the port of Peiraieus, where the first cases were reported in the summer, soon after the Peloponnesians had begun their second invasion of Athenian territory. From Peiraieus the epidemic spread rapidly to the main part of the city.

Hipparete was almost certainly infected by the plague, which did not discriminate between rich and poor in its devastating rampage though the city. Thucydides, who also survived the infection, describes its symptoms in vivid detail. They included a high fever, severe thirst, coughing, stomach pains, retching, uncontrollable diarrhoea and ulcers, both internal and external. Many modern experts have tried to identify the disease from his description, but they have not reached a firm conclusion. It was certainly very contagious and probably killed about one-third of the inhabitants of Athens over a period of about four years, with the worst casualties coming in the first year, when the lack of any acquired immunity made the population particularly vulnerable.

Thucydides tells us that so many people died of the plague, and so quickly, that proper funeral procedures were neglected. Normally Athenian funerals were marked by elaborate private and public rituals, especially in the case of the richer families, who liked to use such occasions to show off their wealth and social status. Preparing the body of the deceased was a duty for the women of the family, who would wash the corpse, anoint it with oil and garland it with flowers. It would be laid on a bier for a day and a night, allowing time for family and friends to mourn and pay their respects. The laws of Athens required the funeral to take place before dawn on the following day. A procession would leave the house of the deceased and go outside the walls of the city, to either a communal or a family cemetery, where the body would be buried or cremated. The men of the family would

lead the procession, with the women walking solemnly behind the corpse and singing a mourning song. When the plague was at its height, however, many bodies were left lying untended, at the mercy of dogs and carrion birds. Others were buried or cremated in haste, sometimes several together, without the proper rituals. Thucydides even describes people carrying corpses around looking for a recently dug grave to drop them in, or an already blazing pyre on which to throw them.

Hipparete was fortunate to have survived the disease, although some members of her father's household must certainly have died, possibly including her mother. We know that her father survived because he was in joint command of an Athenian expedition against the Boiotian city of Tanagra in 426. Her brother Kallias also lived through the infection, but the horrific effects of epidemic will certainly have left a lasting impression on the family. Young Hipparete had no choice but to remain in the city while all this was happening, whereas her father and many of the other men could leave the city on commercial or diplomatic missions, or as part of the military forces sent on raids against the Peloponnesians and their allies. We can be sure that it was a dark and troubled period of her life, as she longed for relief from the anxieties of war, like thousands of other women and girls in the city.

While people doubtless tried to carry on their lives as normally as possible during this period, for many the city must have felt like a living nightmare, comparable to the mythical Tartaros, where the souls of the wicked were subjected to eternal torments and punishments. Thucydides also blames the shattering impact of the plague for a general breakdown in the social structures and moral standards of the Athenians.

The general's wife

One example of the change in moral standards during the war may be the extravagant behaviour of Hipparete's husband, Alkibiades, whom she married in about 424, when she was aged no more than 16. Alkibiades was at least 10 years older than her, as was usual in Classical Athens. He came from one of a group of Athenian families known as the Eupatridai, or noble families. His father, Kleinias, had been killed in the battle of Koroneia in 446. His mother, Deinomache, was a relative by marriage of Perikles and for a time after his father's death Alkibiades lived in the household of Perikles, who, along with his brother Ariphron, was Alkibiades' guardian. Given the closeness of their respective families it is probable that Hipparete would have met her future husband before they were married, but she is unlikely to have spent much time in his company. Athenian marriages were normally arranged between the parents or guardians of the couple and it was not unusual for cousins or even siblings to arrange for their respective children to marry, renewing and strengthening their family ties. In this case it is very likely that there were strong financial considerations on Alkibiades' side, as Hipparete would have brought a substantial dowry to the marriage. There were also political advantages in the match, as her family connections were of the highest order. She would have been seen as the perfect wife for an ambitious young man.

The primary duty of an Athenian wife was to bear children for her husband, preferably a male child, who could inherit his father's property and continue the family line. Hipparete fulfilled this duty by providing her husband with a son, also called Alkibiades, and a daughter, whose name is not known. It is likely that she had another son, but he died in infancy, a common misfortune in ancient times, when medical knowledge was very limited.

In stark contrast to her husband, who participated in diplomatic missions and military campaigns as her father had done, once she was married Hipparete probably rarely travelled beyond the confines of her home. Nor is it likely that Hipparete would have been involved in any of Alkibiades'

activities: Citizen women participated in funerals and certain religious festivals, in some cases as the main celebrants, but otherwise they had no role in the public life of the cities. She will have heard about her husband's wartime adventures and, possibly, discussed them with him, but war and politics were seen as exclusively the concern of men. In a famous speech, which Thucydides puts into the mouth of Perikles, in honour of those who died in the early stages of the war, the only mention of women is a comment addressed to the widows of the fallen, that their greatest glory is not to be talked about by men, whether in praise or criticism.

Hipparete had been brought up to respect and obey the men in her life and she seems to have done all she could to be a good wife, but on at least one occasion her husband's behaviour drove her to attempt to end their marriage. While Athenian men expected their wives to be completely faithful, married men thought nothing of having intercourse with their female slaves, or with prostitutes, who might be slaves or free women from outside Athens. It was even considered acceptable for an unmarried man to keep a concubine in his home, but he would be expected to end such arrangements once he took a wife.

When the Athenians captured the island of Melos in 416 they killed the men and enslaved the women and children. Alkibiades bought one of these unfortunate women and kept her in his household as a concubine, eventually having a son by her. The effect of the Melian slave's presence upon Hipparete must have been devastating. Here was a woman whom her husband had purchased as booty, yet he preferred her to his own well-born wife as his sexual partner. We can imagine that Hipparete might have sympathised with the woman's plight, for if Athens were to be defeated in the war, then she too could expect to be enslaved by the victors. On the other hand, by installing another woman in their home Alkibiades was showing a lack of respect to Hipparete, even though she was the mother of his children and the daughter of a prominent Athenian citizen.

A young hoplite is shown saying goodbye to his family on this Athenian vase, painted around the start of the Peloponnesian War. Men over the age of 50 would not normally be expected to fight, unless there was a shortage of younger, fitter men. The wives and mothers of those who went off to war might have to wait months, or even years before they had news of their loved ones. (Ancient Art and Architecture)

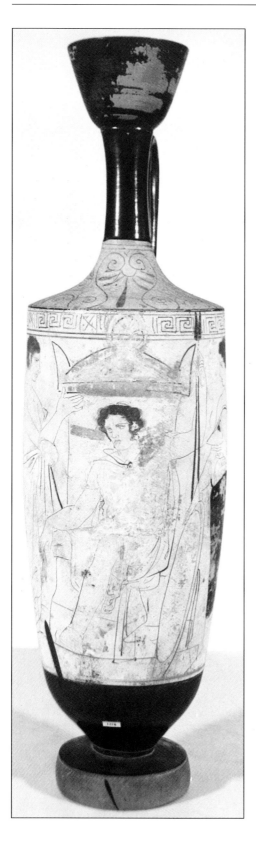

The Athenian white-ground oil jug was painted in the last quarter of the fifth century BC. The artist has chosen to portray a handsome man in front of what seems to be his own tomb, with a young woman and a young man standing on either side. The two spears in man's hand and the shield and helmet held by the woman suggest that he is a deceased hoplite whose wife and brother (or son) are mourning his death. (Ancient Art and Architecture)

It seems to have been this situation that finally induced Hipparete to leave her husband and return to her brother's house, her father having died by this time. An Athenian woman had the right to leave her husband's household if she was being mistreated, and to petition a magistrate to grant legal recognition of the divorce. When Hipparete approached the magistrate, however, Alkibiades himself was there. He dragged her back to his house, where she remained until her death, which occurred soon afterwards. Her life was a not a long one, but at least she did not live to see her husband tried for impiety and forced into exile in Sparta, his property auctioned, and her son threatened with banishment because of his father's political activities. Nor did she witness the bitter end to the war.

The fall of Athens

The defeat of the Athenian expedition to Sicily presented the Spartans and their allies with a golden opportunity to take the initiative in the war. They struck at Athens herself by establishing a permanent fort in Attika at Dekeleia, and they struck at the core of her maritime empire in the Aegean by assembling fleets and either persuading or forcing many of Athens' subject allies to desert her. For the Athenians this new phase of the war produced greater strains, both economic and political. They found it particularly difficult to fund their naval forces as their flow of tribute revenue was interrupted and their pool of naval manpower was diminished. Many of the non-Athenian oarsmen and sailors were attracted away by the higher and more regular pay available to those serving with the Spartans, who now enjoyed the enormous financial backing of the king of Persia. When they needed to assemble a fleet in 406 to rescue their admiral Konon who was blockaded at Mytilene the Athenians had to resort to offering freedom and citizenship to any slaves who would volunteer to row the ships.

One person who had changed sides in the other direction was the exiled Athenian leader Alkibiades. He had found it difficult to settle in at Sparta, where he was forced to swap the extravagant parties beloved of Athenian aristocrats for a tedious round of physical training and the more sombre religious gatherings of the elite Spartan citizens. He accompanied the early Spartan expedition to the Aegean, but as a defector from the enemy he was treated with suspicion, a situation that was not helped by the fact that he had an affair with King Agis' wife while in Sparta. Such suspicions restricted his opportunities for significant involvement in the war and provided no real outlet for his ambitious personality. In 411 he left the Spartan fleet and went to the one remaining centre of power and influence in the war, the Persians.

Oligarchic revolution in Athens

Tissaphernes the Persian satrap decided, possibly at the prompting of Alkibiades to adopt a new strategy in 411. Instead of helping the Spartans defeat the Athenians he would prolong the war between them and take advantage of their conflict to win back some of the Greek cities and islands that had once belonged to the Great King. Alkibiades for his part began plotting to obtain his own recall to Athens by engineering a change in the Athenian government to a more conservative, oligarchic one. He hoped to ingratiate himself with this new regime by offering to use his influence to bring Tissaphernes and the resources of the Persian Empire onto the side of the Athenians. Alkibiades persuaded several of the leading men in the Athenian fleet at Samos to bring about the change of government and in due course a programme of reforms was pushed through the Assembly with the help of a mixture of threats, political assassinations and promises of Persian support. The result was a new Council of 400, replacing the old democratic one of 500 and comprising men wealthy enough to afford their own hoplite equipment. They were charged with drawing up a list of no more than 5,000 Athenian citizens of similar status who would form the decision making body of the new constitution. The idea seems to have been that these men would be wealthy enough not to need payment for carrying out public offices. The 400 made peace overtures to Sparta. Meanwhile Tissaphernes made a new

The figures on the left and in the centre of this gravestone carved
around 410 in Athens represent the deceased men Sosias and
Kephisodoros. The figure on the right is bidding one of his fallen
comrades farewell. As the war dragged on the large numbers of citizen
casualties made many Athenians favour a peaceful settlement with
Sparta. (AKG Berlin)

treaty with the Spartans, so the recall of Alkibiades ceased to be a worthwhile aim.

There was considerable resistance to these developments among the ordinary Athenians in the fleet at Samos. They met in their own version of the citizens' assembly, deposed their current generals and declared their opposition to the new regime. Alkibiades convinced them that he could bring Tissaphernes over to their side and was elected as a general. Back in Athens splits among the 400, a failure to produce the list of 5,000 elite citizens and the failure of negotiations with Sparta caused the regime to lose its credibility. A Spartan attack on Euboia, which prompted the cities there to revolt from Athens, hastened the collapse of the oligarchy. A meeting of an assembly which might be considered to comprise the 5,000 deposed the Council of 400 and voted to recall Alkibiades. Some of the leaders of the oligarchic revolution fled to Dekeleia, others were rounded up, put on trial and condemned to death.

There seems to have followed a brief period in which the Athenian assembly and official posts in the government were restricted to the members of the 5,000. In 410, however, a law was passed which allowed anyone who 'overthrows the democracy or holds any office after the democracy has been overthrown' to be killed without fear of reprisal and his property confiscated. A fund was set up to pay the holders of all public offices. In effect the old democratic constitution was restored.

The final conflicts

The period 410 to 406 was one of almost continuous naval activity in the Eastern Aegean and the Hellespontine region. The struggle for naval supremacy between the two sides eventually decided the outcome of the war. The northern Persian satrap, Pharnabazos, encouraged the Spartans to direct their attention to the Athenian controlled cities in the Hellespont, by offering them subsidies to pay the crews of their ships and troops to support their incursions on

land. The city of Byzantion was won over in 410 by a Peloponnesian fleet led by the Spartan admiral Mindaros. Byzantion's position at the entrance to the Black Sea made it vital to Athenian interests. In addition to much other trade, each year a substantial fleet of ships carrying grain from the Black Sea sailed through the narrow Hellespontine channel that Byzantion protected. The Athenians took two years to recover the city and never managed to completely dislodge the Peloponnesians from the area for the rest of the war. There were several Athenian successes, notably at Kyzikos in 410, when almost the entire Peloponnesian fleet was lost and Mindaros was killed.

A major turning point occurred in 407, when two new leaders took up the struggle against the Athenians. One was a Spartan admiral called Lysandros, who improved the Spartan naval forces dramatically. The other was Kyros, the younger son of the Persian king, who was sent to the western satrapies of the Great King's empire with instructions to make sure that the Spartans won the war. Tissaphernes' strategy had evolved into a balancing act, attempting to keep the opposing Athenian and Peloponnesian forces roughly equal in strength, wearing each other down, until he could make a decisive intervention and drive both sides out of the western satrapies altogether. With the arrival of Kyros, however, this strategy was abandoned in favour of strong support for the Spartans and their allies.

The relationship between Kyros and Lysandros also made a significant difference to the course of the war in the Aegean. It may well be that they each recognised the ambitious streak in the other man and felt comfortable dealing with a kindred spirit. Kyros nurtured dreams of ruling the Persian Empire in place of his brother, Artaxerxes, who was the king's eldest son. Lysandros could not realistically aspire to the Spartan kingship, because he was not closely related to either of the royal families, but he seems to have felt that he could achieve even greater power and influence outside Sparta than the ambitious Spartan commanders Brasidas and Gylippos.

After the Athenian defeat at Aigospotamoi in 405 all their subject allies deserted them, except for the staunchly democratic island of Samos. The Athenians passed a decree giving them Athenian citizenship. It was reconfirmed in 403 when the Athenians and the Samians both overthrew pro-Spartan oligarchic regimes set up by Lysandros. The decree is inscribed here below figures of Athena and Hera, the patron goddesses of Athens and Samos. (Ancient Art and Architecture)

Alkibiades' influence on the war came to an end in 406 when he left the Athenian fleet at Notion and instead of putting one of the other generals in overall command he opted for his helmsman, Antiochos, who was an old friend. Antiochos unwisely tried to catch some of Lysandros' fleet in an ambush and suffered a serious defeat, losing 22 ships. Alkibiades was held responsible but, rather than return to Athens to face the wrath of the Assembly, he went off to some private fortresses he had established in the Hellespont. Lysandros was temporarily replaced by another Spartan admiral, Kallikratidas, who was killed in another Athenian naval victory at the Arginousai Islands in 406. The Athenians largely negated their success by condemning most of their generals to death for failing to do enough to rescue the crews of damaged ships. The Spartans, at Kyros' insistence, restored Lysandros to the command of their fleet. The final decisive battle was fought in the Hellespont late in 405. Lysandros' fleet was besieging the city of Lampsakos and the Athenians beached their ships on the opposite side of the Hellespont at Aigospotamoi. They sailed out for five successive days to try to draw Lysandros into a battle but he stayed put. When the Athenians had returned to their camp on the fifth evening, and their crews were dispersing to look for food, Lysandros attacked, catching them completely by surprise. All but a handful of the Athenian ships were captured. With this victory Lysandros effectively won the war for Sparta.

The Athenians realised that they could not continue their struggle without a strong fleet to give them access to their maritime empire. In the spring of 404 both Spartan kings led armies up to the walls of Athens and Lysandros moored his fleet outside the harbour at Peiraieus. The Athenians waited behind their walls during a tense period of negotiations between the Spartan ephors and an embassy headed by Theramenes. The embassy returned with the news that the Spartans had resisted pressure from her allies, led by Thebes and Corinth, to destroy the city and enslave the citizens. In return the Athenians were required to dismantle their fortifications, surrender all but 12 of their remaining ships and become allies of the Spartans. Lysandros and his fleet sailed into the harbour and immediately set to work demolishing sections of the walls to the accompaniment of flutes. The historian Xenophon, who witnessed this celebration of Spartan victory, wrote in his account: 'They believed this day to be the beginning of freedom for the Greeks.'

The Eastern Aegean and the Hellespont 411–404 BC

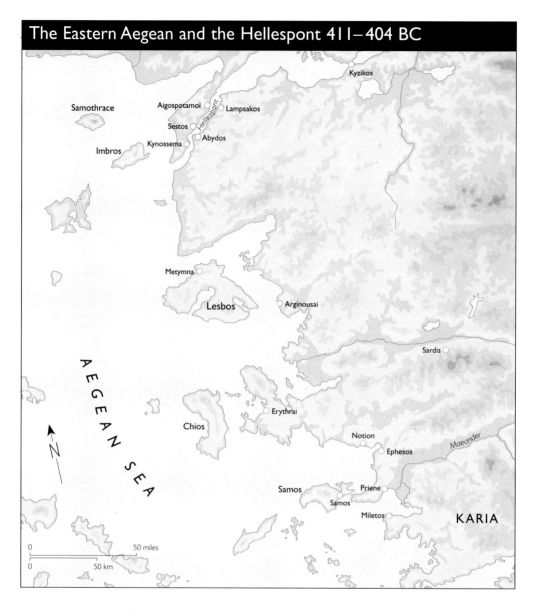

In the latter stages of the Peloponnesian War much of the fighting was concentrated on the cities and islands of the Eastern Aegean and the Hellespont. The Spartans, with Persian help, tried to detach as many places from the Athenian Empire as possible, especially the large islands of Chios, Samos and Lesbos. Control of the Hellespont was vitally important to Athenian maritime trade, particularly in grain; this is why the final, decisive sea battle was fought there.

The triumph of Sparta?

Thucydides blamed the eventual defeat of Athens on her internal political conflicts. Although we do not have his detailed account of the end of the war, he does give us some brief comments on its outcome after his discussion of Perikles' strategy in the early years of the confrontation. He observes that, after their losses in Sicily and the intervention of the Persian king on the Spartan side, the Athenians were still able to continue the war for another eight years. In his words it was, 'not before they had torn themselves apart fighting against each other that they were compelled to surrender.' We have seen several examples of this internal political conflict, the condemnation of Alkibiades, the oligarchic revolution of 411 and the trial and execution of the generals after the battle of Arginousai in 406. It is also clear that sustaining a war that involved so many men and ships put an enormous strain on the resources of a relatively small state. The Spartans were reluctant to commit many of their own citizens to the conflict, but because they were backed up by Persia and a wide coalition of allies they were able to keep the pressure on the Athenians until they ran out of the money and manpower to continue the fight.

After their surrender to the Spartans in 404 the Athenians had to suffer the replacement of their democratic constitution by an oligarchy. This new regime consisted of a board of 30 men whose remit was to draw up a new long-term constitution for Athens. These so-called 'Thirty Tyrants' had

An Athenian silver coin. The design features the owl as a symbol of Athena, goddess of wisdom and the letters ATHE. Lysandros entrusted most of the money plundered from Athens in 404 to Gylippos, who stole some of it and hid it under the tiles of his house. A Helot betrayed him to the ephors by saying that there were a lot of owls roosting under his roof. (Ancient Art and Architecture)

the backing of Lysandros and 700 hoplites
sent by the Spartans. The oligarchs, many of
whom had fled Athens after the failed
revolution in 411 set about settling old
scores and enriching themselves at the
expense of both citizens and non-Athenian
residents like the speech-writer Lysias and
his brother Polemarchos, who were both
arrested on trumped-up charges so that their
property could be confiscated. Some of their
victims fled, like Lysias, who escaped to
Megara, but others, like Polemarchos were
executed. Theramenes, one of the Thirty
tried to oppose this reign of terror, but he
was denounced by his colleague Kritias and
put to death.

Many of Athens' former enemies, such as
Corinth, Megara and Thebes were upset
that Sparta had refused their demands to
punish the Athenians in the way that they
had treated Melos and Skione, by executing
their male citizens and enslaving the
women and children. They also resented
the fact that the Spartans plundered Athens
but did not share the booty. They did not
wish to see Athens become just a subject
ally of Sparta so they gave shelter and
support to the opponents of the Thirty. A
substantial democratic faction under the
leadership of Thrasyboulos returned to
Athens and occupied the Peiraieus. In the
fighting that followed Kritias was killed and
the Spartan king Pausanias intervened to
stop further violence. The remaining
oligarchs and their supporters were granted
a refuge at Eleusis, on the borders of Attika
and the Athenians gradually restored their
full democracy.

The Spartans had won a resounding
victory, but the imposition of an oligarchy

at Athens was just one of a series of
insensitive, arrogant moves which served to
alienate them from their former allies.
Lysandros sent Spartan governors and
garrisons to many of the Greek cities that
had been subject to Athens, as the Spartans
briefly tried to create an empire of their own
out of the fragments of the Athenian one.
They also got drawn into a war with Persia,
partly over their failure to live up to their
side of the agreement that had brought
them Persian financial support, and partly as
a result of the aid they gave to Kyros in his
unsuccessful attempt to overthrow his
brother Artaxerxes, who had become king
on the death of Dareios in 405.

From 396 to about 390 there was an
inconclusive conflict between an alliance of
Greek states, including Corinth, Argos,
Thebes and Athens and the Spartans. This
alliance received both financial and naval
support from the Great King, whose fleet,
commanded by the Athenian admiral
Konon, sailed into Athens in 394 and
restored the sections of the Long Walls that
had been demolished in 404. Eventually the
stalemate was broken by the Spartans who
negotiated another treaty with the king of
Persia in 387/386. This agreement, known as
the King's Peace, proclaimed autonomy for
all the Greeks, except those cities in Asia
Minor that were supposed to have been
returned to Persia under the terms of the
treaty of 411. If anyone broke the terms of
this common peace among the Greeks, then
the Great King would make war on them.
Thus the 'freedom' of the Greeks, that had
been the rallying cry at the start of the
Peloponnesian War, was guaranteed not by
the Spartans, but by the Persian king.

Further reading

Primary sources

Thyucydides, *The Peloponnesian War*, translated by Rex Warner, revised by M. I. Finley, London, Penguin, 1972.

Xenophon, *A History of my Times*, translated by Rex Warner, introduction and notes by G. Cawkwell, London, Penguin, 1979.

Fornara, C. W. (ed.), *From Archaic Times to the End of the Peloponnesian War: Translated Documents of Greece and Rome*, vol I, Cambridge, Cambridge University Press, 1983.

Secondary Sources

Green, P., *Armada from Athens: The Failure of the Sicilian Expedition 415–413 BC*, London, 1970.

Hanson, V. D., *The Western Way of War: Infantry Battle in Classical Greece*, Oxford, 1989.

Kagan, D., *The Outbreak of the Peloponnesian War*, New York, 1969.

Kagan, D., *The Archidamian War*, New York, 1974.

Kagan, D., *The Peace of Nicias and the Sicilian Expedition*, New York, 1981.

Kagan, D., *The Fall of the Athenian Empire*, New York, 1987.

Stainte Croix, G. de, *The Origins of the Peloponnesian War*, London, 1972.

Sealey, R., *A History of the Greek City States 700–338 BC*, Berkely, University of California Press, 1976.

Sekunda. N., and A. McBride, *The Ancient Greeks*, Elite 7, London, Osprey Publishing, 1986.

Spence, I., *The Cavalry of Classical Greece: A Social and Military History with Particular Reference to Athens*, Oxford, 1993.

Index

Related titles from Osprey Publishing

MEN-AT-ARMS (MAA)
**Uniforms, equipment, history
and organisation of troops**

0850455286	MAA 046	THE ROMAN ARMY FROM CAESAR TO TRAJAN
0850452716	MAA 069	THE GREEK AND PERSIAN WARS 500–323 BC
085045333X	MAA 093	THE ROMAN ARMY HADRIAN TO CONSTANTINE
0850453844	MAA 109	ANCIENT ARMIES OF THE MIDDLE EAST
0850454301	MAA 121	ARMIES OF THE CARTHAGINIAN WARS 265–146 BC
0850454735	MAA 129	ROME'S ENEMIES (1) GERMANICS AND DACIANS
0850454786	MAA 137	THE SCYTHIANS 700–300 BC
0850455391	MAA 148	THE ARMY OF ALEXANDER THE GREAT
0850456061	MAA 158	ROME'S ENEMIES (2) GALLIC AND BRITISH CELTS
0850456886	MAA 175	ROME'S ENEMIES (3) PARTHIANS AND SASSANID PERSIANS
0850457017	MAA 180	ROME'S ENEMIES (4) SPANISH ARMIES
0850459427	MAA 218	ANCIENT CHINESE ARMIES 1500–200 BC
1855321661	MAA 243	ROME'S ENEMIES (5) THE DESERT FRONTIER
1855325136	MAA 283	EARLY ROMAN ARMIES
1855325144	MAA 284	IMPERIAL CHINESE ARMIES (1) 200 BC–589 AD
1855325985	MAA 291	REPUBLICAN ROMAN ARMY 200–104 BC
1841763292	MAA 360	THE THRACIANS 700 BC–AD 46
184176485X	MAA 373	THE SARMATIANS 600 BC – AD 450

CAMPAIGN (CAM)
**Strategies, tactics and battle experiences
of opposing armies**

1855321106	CAM 007	ALEXANDER 334–323 C
1855323001	CAM 022	QADESH 1300 BC
1855324709	CAM 036	CANNAE 216 BC

ELITE (ELI)
**Uniforms, equipment, tactics and personalities
of troops and commanders**

085045686X	E L I 007	THE ANCIENT GREEKS
1855321637	E L I 039	THE ANCIENT ASSYRIANS
1855322080	E L I 040	NEW KINGDOM EGYPT
1855322501	E L I 042	THE PERSIAN ARMY 560–330 BC
1855323613	E L I 050	THE PRAETORIAN GUARD
1855326590	E L I 066	THE SPARTAN ARMY

WARRIOR (WAR)
**Motivation, training, combat experiences
and equipment of individual soldiers**

1855328674	WAR 027	GREEK HOPLITE 480–23 BC
1841761435	WAR 030	CELTIC WARRIOR 300 BC–AD 100
1841762997	WAR 039	GLADIATORS 100 BC–AD 200

ESSENTIAL HISTORIES (ESS)
**Concise overviews of major wars
and theatres of war**

1841763551	ESS 016	THE PUNIC WARS 264–146 BC

ORDER OF BATTLE (OOB)
**Unit-by-unit troop movements and
command strategies of major battles**
Contact us for more details – see below

NEW VANGUARD (NVG)
**Design, development and operation
of the machinery of war**
Contact us for more details – see below

To order any of these titles, or for more information on Osprey Publishing, contact:
Osprey Direct (UK)   *Tel:* +44 (0)1933 443863   *Fax:* +44 (0)1933 443849   *E-mail:* info@ospreydirect.co.uk
Osprey Direct (USA) c/o MBI Publishing   *Toll-free:* 1 800 826 6600   *Phone:* 1 715 294 3345
Fax: 1 715 294 4448   *E-mail:* info@ospreydirectusa.com
www.ospreypublishing.com

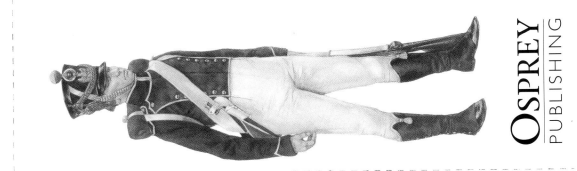

FIND OUT MORE ABOUT OSPREY

❏ Please send me a FREE trial issue of Osprey Military Journal

❏ Please send me the latest listing of Osprey's publications

❏ I would like to subscribe to Osprey's e-mail newsletter

Title/rank _____

Name _____

Address _____

_____

_____

_____

Postcode/zip _____

State/country _____

E-mail _____

Which book did this card come from?

_____

❏ I am interested in military history

My preferred period of military history is _____

❏ I am interested in military aviation

My preferred period of military aviation is _____

I am interested in (please tick all that apply)

❏ general history   ❏ militaria   ❏ model making

❏ wargaming   ❏ re-enactment

Please send to:

USA & Canada:
Osprey Direct USA, c/o MBI Publishing,
PO Box 1, 729 Prospect Ave, Osceola, WI 54020, USA

UK, Europe and rest of world:
Osprey Direct UK, PO Box 140, Wellingborough,
Northants, NN8 2FA, United Kingdom

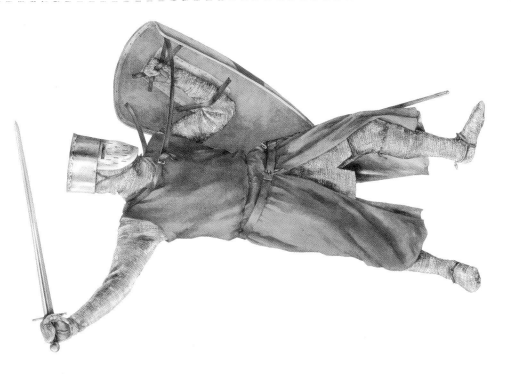

OSPREY
PUBLISHING

www.ospreypublishing.com

call our telephone hotline
for a free information pack

USA & Canada: 1-800-826-6600
UK, Europe and rest of world call:
+44 (0) 1933 443 863

Young Guardsman
Figure taken from *Warrior 22:*
Imperial Guardsman 1799–1815
Published by Osprey
Illustrated by Christa Hook

Knight, c.1190
Figure taken from *Warrior 1: Norman Knight 950 – 1204AD*
Published by Osprey
Illustrated by Christa Hook

POSTCARD